LAST STAND

AT

LE PARADIS

LAST STAND
AT
LE PARADIS

*The Events Leading to the
SS Massacre of the Norfolks 1940*

by

Richard Lane

Pen & Sword
MILITARY

First published in Great Britain in 2009 by
Pen & Sword Military
an imprint of
Pen & Sword Books Ltd
47 Church Street
Barnsley
South Yorkshire
S70 2AS

ISBN 978 1 84415 847 8

A CIP catalogue record for this book is
available from the British Library

Typeset in Sabon by
Phoenix Typesetting, Auldgirth, Dumfriesshire

Printed and bound in England by
CPI UK

Pen & Sword Books Ltd incorporates the Imprints of Pen & Sword Aviation,
Pen & Sword Maritime, Pen & Sword Military, Wharncliffe Local History,
Pen & Sword Select, Pen & Sword Military Classics and Leo Cooper.

For a complete list of Pen & Sword titles please contact
PEN & SWORD BOOKS LIMITED
47 Church Street, Barnsley, South Yorkshire, S70 2AS, England
E-mail: enquiries@pen-and-sword.co.uk
Website: www.pen-and-sword.co.uk

In loving memory of my husband

Richard Lane

7 October 1947 – 25 August 2008

'A life well spent and thoroughly enjoyed'

Debbi Lane
October 2008

'I wish I could write and tell the story of the unselfish heroism of those men who fought, and laughed, and died without complaint although they knew they had no chance of getting home, and that all they could do was to fight to the end and give time to others to get home instead. Frankly, I love them and their unconscious gallantry so very much, what I imagine their fathers must have shown in the great retreat from Mons and in the Salient in the last great war.'

From a letter written by one of the company commanders, who was taken prisoner on the final day.

History of The Royal Norfolk Regiment, 1919–1951, vol. III, by Lieutenant Commander P.K. Kemp.

CONTENTS

THE ROYAL NORFOLK REGIMENT

IN THE 274 YEARS OF ITS EXISTENCE, the 9th of Foot, which became the Royal Norfolk Regiment, served with distinction throughout much of the world. Raised in 1685 by King James II as one of eight new regiments formed to combat Monmouth's Rebellion, it was known as Colonel Henry Cornwall's Regiment of Foot.

Although it took no part in the actual crushing of the rebellion, the subsequent story of the Regiment is a microcosm of world history: of new nations being forged, old nations tearing themselves apart, and of the policing of a vast and very diverse Empire.

Men of the 9th fought and died in King William's Irish Campaign, the War of the Spanish Succession, the American War of Independence, the Peninsular War, the Crimean War, the South African (Boer) War, the First World War, the Second World War and Korea. Protection of colonial interests took its soldiers to the West Indies, Canada, India, Afghanistan and Cyprus. At times, climatic conditions were harsh and the resultant diseases killed more men than conflict.

From 1747 onwards, it was known as the 9th Regiment of Foot; then in 1782 it became the 9th or East Norfolk Regiment. Seventeen years later, on 30 July 1799, H. Calvert, the Adjutant-General, wrote to Lieutenant General Bertie, the Colonel of the Regiment, stating that: 'I have received His Royal Highness the Commander-in-Chief's directions to signify to you that His Majesty has been pleased to confirm to the Ninth Regiment of Foot the distinction and privilege of bearing the figure of "Britannia" as the badge of the Regiment.' According to tradition, however, the badge was originally granted by Queen Anne because of the gallantry the Regiment displayed at the Battle of Almanza in 1707.

Out of this singular honour arose the nickname the 'Holy Boys'. The story goes that during the Peninsular War (1808–1814), the Spanish population mistook the image of Britannia for a representation of the Virgin Mary. Another, somewhat less flattering soubriquet was the 'Hungry Ninth' stemming from an incident where the men sold their bibles in order to buy food and wine.

In 1881, the 9th became The Norfolk Regiment. Royal was granted in 1935 to commemorate both the Silver Jubilee and birthday of King George V. It was also the 250th anniversary of the raising of the Regiment.

For King and Country has long been the patriotic call to arms in times of major conflict. In the two world wars of the twentieth century, citizen soldiers in the form of conscripts had to answer that call. Those who entered the Army found themselves in regiments whose histories, like the Norfolks, stretched back to the seventeenth century and even beyond. Proud traditions had been forged on the battlefields of Europe, America and Asia, by men who were professionals, whose life despite the hardships and savage discipline, was military service. To them, those endless ghostly columns, the Regiment was home and family, a unique bond of brotherhood that only soldiers know.

The ghostly columns may remain, tramping their way across the blood-spattered fields of history, but so many of the regiments they served have themselves become spectres. The end for the Holy Boys came in 1959 as the Government reduced the number of units in the British Army. The Norfolks were amalgamated with the 12th of Foot, the Suffolk Regiment, to form the 1st East Anglian Regiment. During the years that followed further amalgamations brought other old East Anglian regiments together to create The Royal Anglian Regiment.

Of the thousands who have served the 9th of Foot throughout its long and distinguished history, it is the story of those men of the 2nd Battalion who marched into France at the outbreak of the Second World War that is told in these pages. They were regulars, professionals to a man, many of whom had been reservists, recalled to the colours after a period back in civilian life.

Their campaign was short, violent and tragic. During the final days, beside the Canal d'Aire, they faced overwhelming odds.

They did their utmost to do what was asked of them, often above and beyond the call of duty. In the end, they were sacrificed so that others could get away.

ACKNOWLEDGEMENTS

A BOOK OF THIS NATURE IS REALLY a work of multiple authors. All I have done is to try and construct as detailed an account as possible by bringing together material from many different sources, both published and unpublished, as told by those men who took part.

Interviews conducted by the Imperial War Museum and recorded for posterity in the Sound Archive provide an invaluable source of eyewitness material. From transcriptions and copies of the recordings, some of which are held at the Royal Norfolk Regimental Museum in Norwich, I have featured the recollections of Brigadier Francis Peter Barclay DSO MC (Captain, commanding 'A' Company); Dennis Boast (Private, Carrier Platoon, HQ Company, who joined the Battalion after Dunkirk); Arthur Brough (Mortar Platoon, HQ Company); Bob Brown (Signaller, HQ Company); Ernie Farrow (Private, Pioneer Section, HQ Company); Walter Gilding (Sergeant, Mortar Platoon, HQ Company, then Company Quartermaster Sergeant); Ernie Leggett (Private 'A' Company); Herbert Lines (Carrier Platoon, HQ Company), and Bill Seymour (Corporal, who joined the Battalion after Dunkirk).

For those who may wish to make a further study of these first-hand accounts, the Imperial War Museum accession numbers are given as a footnote to the chapter in which each of the men first appears.

My thanks to Mr David Bell of the Imperial War Museum for permission to quote the extracts, and to those members of the museum staff who, over a number of years, have compiled such an invaluable record of wartime experiences.

From the written record: Ernie Farrow's story is also told by Cyril Jolly in *The Man Who Missed The Massacre*, 1986. Albert

Pooley's and William O'Callaghan's stories are told by Cyril Jolly in *The Vengeance of Private Pooley* (1956); I am grateful to Mrs Deborah Duncan, her mother and sister, for permission to quote from the late Mr Jolly's work.

Lieutenant Colonel C. R. Murray Brown DSO provided an account of the 2nd Battalion's operations in France for the *Britannia Magazine*, No. 27.

D.E. Jones wrote of his experiences in a letter held at the Royal Norfolk Regimental Museum, Norwich.

Charles Long MC, appointed Adjutant of the Battalion on 21 May 1940, complied two accounts while a prisoner of war. Written in note form, they give a daily digest of operations, although his timings of events towards the end of the Battle of La Bassée differ from those given in the 4th Infantry Brigade War Diary. 'A War Diary' covers the period from the German invasion on 10 May until 28 May.

'Report on Battle of La Bassée 24–28 May 1940' overlaps 'A War Diary' but gives a more detailed account of the last four days. At the end of the report, Charles Long lists those officers, all prisoners of war at Oflag VI/B, Warberg, Germany who assisted him with information. By way of tribute the listing is repeated here: Captain Stokes, 61st Medium Regiment, Royal Artillery; Lieutenant Nelson, 13th Anti-Tank Regiment, Royal Artillery; fellow Royal Norfolk officers, Captains Gordon and Hallett, Lieutenant Woodwark and Second Lieutenants Elson and Simpson; Captain Hastings, Oxfordshire and Buckinghamshire Light Infantry on attachment to the Royal Norfolks; Major Bruce, 1st Royal Scots; Major Eaton, 1/8th Lancashire Fusiliers; Captain Errington, 1st Royal Scots and Second Lieutenants Spears and Verity, 1/8th Lancashire Fusiliers. Both these accounts are in the Royal Norfolk Regimental Museum, Norwich.

I am greatly indebted to the Trustees of the museum for allowing me to quote at length from all the above material held in their archive, including the books *The Royal Norfolk Regiment* by Tim Carew (The Royal Norfolk Regiment Association, 1991) and *History of The Royal Norfolk Regiment 1919–1951*, vol. III (Soman Wherry Press, 1953).

The German view of the Battle of La Bassée is drawn from the testimony of those men who gave evidence during the Le Paradis

War Crimes Trial and Investigation. A full transcript of this is held at the Royal Norfolk Regimental Museum in Norwich.

I must thank all the following for permission to quote extracts from their publications: Peter Franzen OBE, editor *Eastern Daily Press*, Norwich; Dilip Sarkar author of *Guards VC Blitzkrieg 1940* (Ramrod Publications, 1999); Constable and Robinson from *The Ironside Diaries* (1962), edited by R. MacLeod and Dennis Kelly; from *The Memoirs of General Lord Ismay* by Lord Ismay (William Heinemann Ltd) reprinted by permission of The Random House Group Ltd; the Controller of The Stationery Office and the Queen's Printer for Scotland for *History of The Second World War: Grand Strategy*, vol. I, by N. H. Gibbs (HMSO, 1976) Crown Copyright; The National Archive for 'Lord Gort's Despatches 1939–40 France and Belgium', CAB 120 247 PRO; Leo Cooper for two essays by Peter Caddick-Adams, 'The German Breakthrough at Sedan, 12–15 May l940' and 'Anglo-French Cooperation during the Battle of France', both from *The Battle For France and Flanders Sixty Years On*, editors Professor Brian Bond and Michael Taylor (2001); also to Leo Cooper from *Chief of Staff: the Diaries of Lieutenant General Sir Henry Pownall*, vol. I, edited by Brian Bond (1972); from *Fall of France: The Nazi Invasion of 1940* by Julian Jackson (2003) by permission of Oxford University Press; David Highams Associates for *War Diaries 1939–1945: Field Marshal Lord Alanbrooke*, editors Alex Danchev and Daniel Todman (Orion, 2002); from *The Second World War* by John Keegan (Hutchinson, 1989) reprinted by permission of The Random House Group Ltd; from *Dunkirk: Fight To The Last Man* (Viking, 2004) reproduced with permission of Curtis Brown Ltd, on behalf of Hugh Sebag-Montefiore, copyright Hugh Sebag-Montefiore; The History Press for *Panzer Battles* by Major General F. W. von Mellenthin (Tempus) and *Hitler's Praetorians: The History of the Waffen SS 1925–1945* by Tim Ripley (Spellmount, 2004); to A.P. Watt on behalf of Viscount Montgomery of Alamein for extracts from *The Memoirs of Field Marshal Viscount Montgomery* (Pen and Sword, 2007).

Every effort has been made to contact rights holders to obtain permission to quote extracts from their work. In a few cases this has not been possible.

Last, but by no means least, my special thanks goes to Kate

Thaxton, Curator of The Royal Norfolk Regimental Museum and one of her volunteers, Dickie Bird, for the many pleasant hours I have spent in their company during the research. Not only are they extremely helpful but whenever coffee was made I was always included.

The museum is housed in the Shire Hall and stands in the shadow of Norwich Castle at the foot of the great mound constructed by the Normans. Considering the resources available, it houses a remarkable collection and provides a fitting tribute to a fine old regiment, a regiment of which the people of Norfolk can be justifiably proud.

Richard Lane
July 2008

The final phases of Richard's book sadly fell to me. I must therefore thank Brigadier Henry Wilson and Bobby Gainher for their support, understanding and encouragement in helping me to complete them.

I must also thank our niece, Hannah Lane, whose help in the proofreading has been invaluable, and was done with much understanding and patience.

I sincerely hope that the finished book, which took Richard four years to complete, will be a fitting tribute to my husband's memory.

Debbi Lane
October 2008

Author's Note

In Belgium, road signs now give the names of towns and villages in Flemish which would certainly have been unfamiliar to the soldiers of both world wars. Ypres, for example, Wipers to the Tommies, is now signed as Ieper. In the text, I have used place and river names as they were known to the British Army, but where there may now be alternatives in use these are given in brackets.

LAST STAND
AT
LE PARADIS

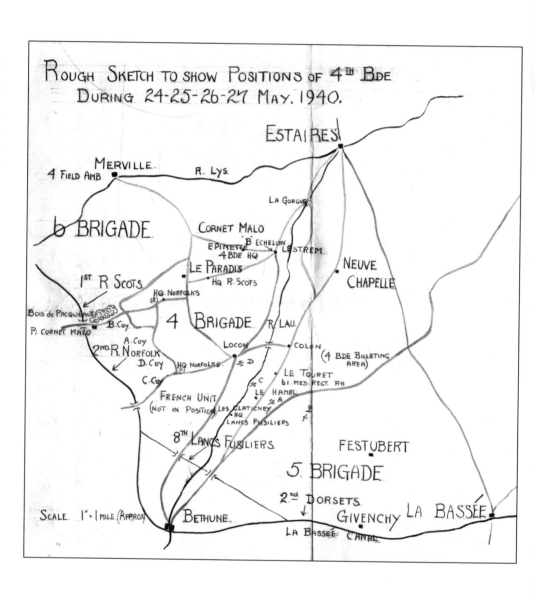

INTRODUCTION

'Come on, let's be getting over there.'

On Monday, 27 May 1940, a day which saw the evacuation of 7,669 men of the British Expeditionary Force from the mole at Dunkirk, the 2nd Battalion Royal Norfolk Regiment was some 35 miles to the south. In a bid to stall the rapid German advance on the line of the Canal d'Aire (La Bassée Canal), the depleted ranks of the Battalion were fighting a desperate rearguard in the villages of Le Cornet Malo, Locon and Le Paradis.

According to the Battalion's Adjutant, Captain Charles Long, the Norfolks received their last message from 4th Infantry Brigade Headquarters at 1640 in the afternoon. It stated: 'You are to hold on till dusk. If possible and if any of you are left you may then withdraw to N.E. to La Nouvelle France – cross water – you will be met and guided.'[1] But the Holy Boys were facing a hopeless situation: German tanks and infantry were across the canal in strength, ammunition was low, manpower decimated and the hours of daylight in May were long. Isolated and surrounded, Battalion Headquarters at Duriez Farm, Le Paradis, was forced to surrender.

The Royal Norfolks, along with the remainder of the 2nd Infantry Division, 'had indeed been sacrificed to keep open the line of retirement to the Lys and delay the junction of the two German army groups which would have cut off all of the French First Army'.[2]

Today, it is no less a moving experience to visit the area of the Pas de Calais where the Holy Boys made their last stand. The inter-

1

vening decades have healed the bloody scars torn into this rich farmland, shattered homes have long since been rebuilt and new generations born who live in the hope that they will never have to suffer the destructive madness which twice erupted during the twentieth century.

Tucked away behind the church of Le Paradis, over 150 neat headstones of the Commonwealth War Graves Commission Cemetery provide a poignant reminder of the human cost, of lives that can never be relived. But this quiet unassuming village holds a much darker memory of the fortunes of armed conflict; of what happens when the rules, those by which nations seek to civilize the ugly brutality of war, are ignored.

Two memorials – one beside the church and the other outside the village on the boundary of a meadow – commemorate ninety-seven men of the BEF, most of them Royal Norfolks, who were shown no mercy by their SS captors. Shortly after the surrender of Battalion Headquarters on that fateful May afternoon, the survivors, wounded amongst them, were marched to a meadow belonging to Monsieur Louis Creton. As they passed in front of the red-brick wall of a farm building, two heavy machine-guns raked the columns of helpless, unarmed men.

In the fullness of time, justice was sought and won for those who perished in this callous act. Ninety-nine men had marched into the deadly storm of 200 bullets but unbeknown to the German perpetrators two men miraculously survived.

Across that final battlefield, other Norfolks were treated in accordance with 'the laws and usages of war', and taken into captivity. Just a handful, numbering five officers and 134 other ranks, had returned to Britain on 7 June to fight again. The Battalion had marched into France almost a thousand strong.

Only twenty-six years before, it had been the Regiment's 1st Battalion which,[3] as part of that 'contemptible little army', had been forced to fall back in the face of a German offensive through Belgium. In May 1940, it was almost as if history was repeating itself, but this time the outlook was bleak – the Allied Army was facing defeat. The BEF was grimly fighting its way to the Channel coast and evacuation.

In the space of two decades, Germany had risen from the ruination of defeat, to bring war back to those areas of Belgium and

France that had scarcely had time to recover from the devastation and slaughter of the last.

After the guns had fallen silent in 1918, a war-wary world demanded lasting peace. Hardly a family had been untouched in some way or other by the First World War. Although a global conflict, images of the Western Front captured on film, canvas and in the words of the soldier poets became indelibly imprinted onto millions of minds: of water-logged trenches; barbed-wire entanglements; the shell-cratered killing ground of no man's land; the sinister clouds of choking, blinding, lung-burning gas; and the heavy casualties, not just those killed but those permanently shattered in mind and body.

The Paris Peace Conference of 1919 and the signing of the Treaty of Versailles, which severely restricted the size of the German armed forces and the weaponry available to them, seemed to offer the prospect of a peaceful future. The threat posed by German militarism had been removed by a few strokes of the pen.

Perceval Landon, writing in the *Daily Telegraph* on 30 June 1919, believed that the world could now expect a generation of peace with 'a hope rising, during that generation, to a higher plane, and so far as human effort can attain that end, looks forward to the end of warfare itself'.

The rise to power of Adolf Hitler soon began the erosion of such optimism. He openly rebuilt his armed forces and in March 1936 reoccupied the Rhineland, a zone demilitarized under the Treaty of Versailles. Sabres were rattled but never unsheathed, and while Winston Churchill consistently warned of the danger posed by a resurgent and rearmed Germany, the French and British simply appeased the dictator's demands.

Well informed as he was regarding the situation in Nazi Germany, Churchill was, at the time, a voice in the political wilderness. And yet his information came from government sources, supposedly unauthorized. Governments, moreover, that appeared loath to tell the unpalatable truth that Germany really was becoming a major threat, and if there should be a war, Britain was ill-prepared to be involved.

In the years following the First World War, Britain's zeal for disarmament had seriously compromised military capability. In March 1932, a year before Hitler was appointed Chancellor of

Germany, the weakness of Britain's military strength was acknowledged; rearmament was discussed but that was as far as it went. Those who subsequently foresaw the threat posed by a resurgent Germany were faced with the difficulty of trying to convince a public which would not countenance another war, and would simply dismiss them as warmongers.

Accusations of warmongering had been made against the National Coalition Government by the Labour Party during the election of 1935. That the Government was sensitive about this issue is evident from remarks made in the House of Commons by Prime Minister, Stanley Baldwin, on 12 November 1936.

'Supposing,' he said, 'I had gone to the country and said that Germany was rearming, and that we must rearm, does anybody think that this pacific democracy would have rallied to that cry at that moment? I cannot think of anything that would have made the loss of the election from my point of view more certain.'

Baldwin, it appears, was placing his own electoral ambitions above the security of the nation, a view that Churchill was not afraid to express openly.

A five-year rearmament programme had, however, been agreed early in 1936. With Germany forging well ahead, it has been argued that both Baldwin and his successor, Neville Chamberlain, who became Prime Minister in May 1937, were attempting to buy time to rearm with the policy of appeasement. Besides, rearmament was an expensive business, redirecting money which Chamberlain felt could be better spent on social welfare, an issue he feared might cost him the next election and bring the Labour Party to power. Party political considerations aside, Chamberlain was facing a difficult situation. Because of the low level of Britain's military capability, he was warned that the country was in no position to fight a war against Germany, a war which would probably involve Italy and Japan as well. Despite the size and reputation of the French Army, Chamberlain was very sceptical about the reliability of the French, who he arrogantly considered spineless. Neither could he rely on transatlantic assistance as the United States of America was determined not to become embroiled in another European War.

In March 1938, Austria was absorbed into the Reich. Hitler informed the outside world that Austria was the last of his annexations, but his mind was firmly set on Czechoslovakia and the three million Germans living in the border region, the Sudetenland. In August, he set October as the date for military action in support of the Sudeten Germans. At a Nazi Party rally in September, he said: 'my demand is that the oppression of three and a half million Germans in Czechoslovakia shall cease and its place shall be taken by the free right of self-determination. We should be sorry if, through this, our relations to the other European states should be troubled or suffer damage. But in that case the fault would not be ours.'

A diplomatic solution was sought at the Munich Conference held from 28 to 30 September. The leaders of Britain, France, Italy and Germany decided the fate of Czechoslovakia without a representative of that country being present. The Sudetenland was to become part of Germany but the remaining Czech frontiers were to be respected.

Neville Chamberlain returned to London brandishing, for the press photographers and newsreel cameras, a piece of paper on which was typed a joint declaration. Signed by both the Prime Minister and the Führer, it expressed the desire of the two countries never to go to war. Chamberlain reassured the British people that he believed it was 'peace for our time . . . peace with honour'. To others including Winston Churchill it was defeat.

Peaceful reassurances there may have been but the Munich Conference actually marked the end of appeasement. Chamberlain and his French counterpart, Daladier knew that rearmament had to continue at speed. In conceding to Hitler's demands, the prospect of war had been delayed. The time would come when the Allies would have to show their military strength and, despite Chamberlain's claims of peace, the British people were beginning to accept the inevitability of another war.

Six months later, on 15 March 1939, German troops crossed the remaining Czech borders and entered the capital, Prague. The following day, at 1915, Hitler arrived in Prague and took up residence in Hradzin Castle.

Two days later, Chamberlain issued a clear warning that Britain would resist any further aggression against smaller states. The French, too, agreed that Germany had to be stopped. Hitler, however, neither believed nor feared these threats.

'History,' he had declared in *Mein Kampf*, 'teaches us that nations which have once given way before the threat of arms without being forced to do so will accept the greatest humiliation and exactions rather than make a fresh appeal to force.'

Confident in his theory, the Führer pressed on with his belligerent foreign policy. In March, he demanded that the former German port of Memel on the Baltic (today Klaipeda), which had been administered as an autonomous region by Lithuania since 1923, be returned to the Fatherland. The Lithuanians promptly gave way and the port was occupied by the Germans on the 23rd.

The menacing shadow of the Reich was also hovering over another of its eastern neighbours, over territory which, under the peace settlement of 1919, had been granted to Poland. Hitler accused the Poles of interfering with German access to East Prussia through the Danzig Corridor (today Danzig is Gdansk), a strip of Polish territory separating East Prussia from the rest of Germany. As usual, the Nazis had their sympathizers in the region agitating for incorporation into the Reich.

In the immediate aftermath of the occupation of Memel, Britain and France announced that they would defend Belgium, Holland and Switzerland against German aggression, a guarantee that was extended to Poland on 31 March, 'to lend the Polish Government all the support in their power'.

A week later, Mussolini, in imitation of his German Ally, annexed Albania, and the Franco-British Alliance issued further guarantees to Romania and Greece on 13 April.

In August, the strategic situation changed dramatically. On the 23rd, Germany signed a non-aggression pact with the Soviet Union while at the same time secretly agreeing to the partition of Eastern Europe. If the announcement came as a surprise to the Western Allies, who were hoping for their own deal with Stalin, it came as a huge surprise to many Soviet citizens who regarded Germany as their arch-enemy. There were those in Britain who now thought that the pact provided an excuse to abandon the obligation made at the end of March to support Poland. But Chamberlain was quick to point out that it 'is our first duty to remove any such dangerous illusion'.

A message from Chamberlain's Government was conveyed directly to Adolf Hitler by the British Ambassador but was contemptuously rejected.

'Such a response,' said the *Daily Telegraph* on 25 August, 'makes it too evident that the reiterated invitation to resort to negotiation as an alternative to war falls in Germany on deaf ears'.

In the early hours of Friday, 1 September, German forces swept across the Polish borders. Two days later, at 1115, Neville Chamberlain addressed the nation in a radio broadcast from the Cabinet Room at 10 Downing Street:

> This morning, the British Ambassador in Berlin handed the German Government a final Note stating that, unless we heard from them by eleven o'clock that they were prepared at once to withdraw their troops from Poland, a state of war would exist between us.
>
> I have to tell you now that no such undertaking has been received, and that consequently this country is at war with Germany.

At 1640 on Sunday, 3 September 1939, some five and a half hours after Chamberlain's momentous broadcast, and twenty minutes before the French announced their declaration of war against Germany, the 2nd Battalion Royal Norfolk Regiment received the order to mobilize. Since returning from a posting to Gibraltar in January, the Battalion had undergone intensive training while based at Bordon Camp and then at Oxney.

William O'Callaghan of the Signals Section remembered the moment they were told about the declaration. Shortly after he had completed guard duty an order was issued for the Battalion to assemble in a meadow. Lieutenant Colonel Eric Hayes, the Commanding Officer, then announced that they were at war.

'It was not a speech,' wrote Cyril Jolly, 'it was not an attempt to rouse passions, but the calmly spoken words stirred all sorts of emotions in the hearts of the men.'[4]

According to Captain Peter Barclay,[5] commander of 'A' Company, Hayes was a very astute man who had spoken about the possibility of war a year earlier during the summer of 1938:

> We were stationed at Gibraltar at the time and he summoned the officers to a meeting one afternoon at two o'clock . . . In this talk he made it quite clear that he considered that war –

European war but possibly a global war – would break out in the foreseeable future within, certainly, the next eighteen months . . .

He said things were brewing up to a war, the way things were being conducted in Germany. He thought they were going to overstep their boundaries and in that case we'd undoubtedly be involved and we'd got to be a jolly sight more prepared for it than we were already . . .

And from then on we would have to intensify our training and there would be periods in the evening of lectures to bring us more up to date with modern techniques.

Although they were a regular battalion whose manpower was professional, the Norfolks still had to be brought up to full strength. Men were recalled who, after seven years service, had returned to civilian life and been placed on the reserve list. Signallers Albert Pooley and William O'Callaghan were reservists who had been recalled in August. On the day war was declared, some 3,000 men on the British Army Reserve were 'recalled to the colours' to serve their various regiments once again.

Captain Barclay considered the reservists to be:

a marvellous contingent of trained men, most of whom had only recently left the battalion . . . They fitted straight in because they had been thoroughly trained during the seven years they'd done with the colours and because . . . most of them hadn't been out of the army for long. They just fitted back into their slots without any problem. I remember no difficulty at all in bringing the standard up to, really, the top immediately after they arrived, and we had a very short time before they went to France.

He also thought that many of them were glad to be back with the Battalion. For some it may well have been true, but not all were happy to leave good civilian jobs and settled family lives. Private Ernie Leggett of 'A' Company[6] had this to say:

They didn't react in a bad way. They were pleased to be back with comrades who they knew . . . They talked about civilian life and how they were getting on; some of them were happily in work, good jobs, but regardless of what job they were in they had to come back; some of them had been married, a settled life. Most of them thought it unfair . . . We sympathized with them, it was a terrible thing really to be called back.

Sadly, many of those men never returned to their places of work or saw their families again.

One unlucky NCO never even had time to leave the camp before he was 'recalled to the colours'. Lance Corporal Mason, who bore the nickname 'Mis' or 'Misler', completed his seven years service two days before war was declared and was awaiting transfer to the reserve.

'We all went down to Fleet to celebrate his "demob",' explained Private Ernie Farrow.[7] They had saved some money and so were able to enjoy several beers. When they returned to camp they all went to Misler's tent where he gave away all the clothes he thought he no longer needed. 'We'd all scrounged different things off him. But in the early morning the orderly sergeant came round, found his tent and said: "'Misler', hand your civvies in and draw your uniform out!" Everything had been cancelled so poor "Misler" had to start to be a soldier again.'

By 10 September, full mobilization was complete, and the Holy Boys received a message of congratulations on the smoothness with which it had all been carried out from Brigadier Gammel.

Captain Barclay spoke of his 'admiration about the way it was conducted. There was endless documentation about what was to be carried out in the various stages of the proceedings. We had a very efficient Adjutant . . . Major Marshall and it all went like clockwork. Every day, everybody knew what had to be done.'

Also on the 10th, the Norfolks were visited by Major General H.C. Lloyd, the General Officer Commanding 2nd Infantry Division. He told the men 'that they would be among the first British soldiers to cross the Channel and proceed to the front'.[8]

Movement orders were received on 13 September and a small advance party left Oxney Camp for Southampton. On the 16th, the Battalion's motor transport, consisting of seventy-eight vehicles, under the command of Major E.C. Prattley, departed for

Avonmouth where they embarked for St Nazire. On the 20th, the remainder of the Battalion set off for Southampton.

Barclay reckoned that the Battalion's strength was around 950:

> It was a cracking good fighting machine, there's no doubt about that. We'd been very well trained. The companies individually were well founded with officers and senior NCOs. We worked remarkably well as a team because we'd got a good skipper [Lieutenant Colonel Hayes]. And we did a lot of training while we were in England and able to do battalion training and large-scale formation training . . . We were welded into a very effective unit, there's no doubt about that at all.

The men, too, seemed confident that they could handle the German Army. Their attitude since war had been declared was summed up by Signaller Bob Brown: 'Come on, let's be getting over there . . . We thought we were the top, we had nothing to fear at all . . . We found out in 1940 that we were over-confident.'[9]

As the troops embarked at Southampton they knew they were the spearhead of a British Expeditionary Force which was once again on its way to France to face a German threat. Only twenty-five years and one month had passed since their forebears of 1914 had crossed the Channel to face the Kaiser's Army.

Notes

1. Long, Captain Charles, 'Report on the Battle of La Bassée Canal 24–28 May 1940'. Compiled by Long with the assistance of other officers while POWs at Oflag VI/B, Germany; reproduced by kind permission of the Trustees of the Royal Norfolk Regimental Museum, Norwich.
2. Ellis, L.F., *The War in France and Flanders, 1939 –40*, HMSO, London, 1953.
3. From 1881, it was The Norfolk Regiment; Royal was granted by King George V in 1935.
4. Jolly, Cyril, *The Vengeance of Private Pooley*, Heinemann, 1956; reproduced by courtesy of the Estate of Cyril Jolly.
5. Imperial War Museum, Sound Archive; Peter Barclay's interview, accession number 008192/07.
6. Imperial War Museum, Sound Archive; Ernie Leggett's interview, accession number 17761.
7. Imperial War Museum, Sound Archive; Ernie Farrow's interview, accession number 11479/5.

8. Kemp, Lieutenant Commander P.K., *History of The Royal Norfolk Regiment 1919–1951*, vol. III, Soman Wherry Press, 1953; reproduced by kind permission of the Trustees of the Royal Norfolk Regimental Museum, Norwich.
9. Imperial War Museum, Sound Archive; Bob Brown's interview, accession number 10393/3.

CHAPTER 1

'Our own army is just a little one . . .'

IN THE EARLY HOURS OF THURSDAY, 21 September 1939, the MVs *Royal Daffodil* and *Royal Sovereign* slid into the harbour at Cherbourg. Blacked out to merge into the dark seascape and shepherded by destroyer escorts, the vessels had made the overnight crossing from Southampton without incident.

On board were the men of 2nd Royal Norfolks who, alongside 1st Battalion The Royal Scots and 1st/8th Battalion The Lancashire Fusiliers formed the 4th Infantry Brigade of the 2nd Infantry Division. But the Holy Boys were, in the words of the Regimental History, 'the first complete infantry unit of the BEF to land in France'. The 1st and 2nd Infantry Divisions formed I Corps, the spearhead corps of the British Army.

At Cherbourg the Battalion entrained onto what Bob Brown described as 'the old French cattle trucks' for the rail journey to the brigade assembly area near Noyen-sur-Sarthe, south-west of Le Mans. Their billets were in the Commune of Pirmil. Private Ernie Farrow, on the other hand, said that they travelled directly to Rubempré near Amiens.

For Captain Barclay, it was a complete anti-climax. 'We were bristling to go,' he recalled, 'and instead of that we hung around Le Mans for about a fortnight; no enemy air opposition, let alone ground opposition and . . . before long we were helping farmers with their harvest [while] waiting for the next stage of the proceedings.'

Assisting the local farmers was a good public relations exercise and helped ease any tension there may initially have been. Barclay felt that there was a certain amount of mistrust at first but 'we left a very friendly population in the vicinity.'

This was echoed by the men. Herbert Lines said that they got on 'quite well really with the French civilians.'[1]

Bob Brown found that the older French people, those who had been through the First World War, were very friendly. They wanted the British soldiers to sing some of the old songs such as 'Pack up your Troubles in your Old Kit Bag', 'It's a Long Way to Tipperary', and 'Keep the Home Fires Burning'.

'They remembered all of them,' he said, 'and some could even join in the singing. We had some very good evenings with them.'

There were also cultural differences to get used to. Barclay, who prided himself on knowing the men of his company 'individually jolly well', underestimated a growing taste for things French. He considered them to be 'terribly conservative . . . the beer wasn't the right sort of beer and the French cooking, by and large, was too oily or whatever. They took a long time to get used to anything other than their customary victuals.' He also said that they did not touch wine. 'They didn't take to that at all kindly. Calvados occasionally if they were feeling flush.'

With some this may have been the case but Ernie Leggett painted a different picture.

'French beer,' he said, 'didn't taste like beer, it was a little bit vinegary to me. We started to drink wine.' The wine the French drank was not the medium sweet that some of the men had tasted back home. 'It was a sort of bitter wine, but I got used to it and I got a nice habit for it. I started to drink wine all the time: red wine. They drank it and we thought: "Well, if they can drink it why shouldn't we?"'

The Regimental History records that the Battalion was in the Le Mans area until 28 September, when it began its move to the brigade concentration area at Monchy-Le- Preux just east of Arras.

'We weren't taking any defensive positions or anything,' explained Bob Brown. 'We were just more or less getting straight, getting settled in and getting equipment fixed up and making sure we were in fighting order, as you might say. We were there a few days, perhaps a week.'

Five days later, the Battalion moved forward to relieve the French 201st Regiment d'Infanterie on the Franco-Belgian border, taking over positions in front of the French village of Rumegies. Lieutenant Colonel C.R. Murray Brown DSO, then a Second

Lieutenant, described the area as 'a part of the line consisting for the most part of a 'defended post' on the road crossing the frontier, and a dilapidated fort.'[2]

The men were accommodated in barns and the officers in farm-houses.

'There was no shortage of that type of accommodation,' said Barclay, 'and we could keep our sub-units together as a whole; I mean, at least one platoon had a barn. Sometimes there were two platoons to a barn and then farmhouses in the immediate vicinity were locations of company commanders and platoon commanders . . . We had a company sort of headquarters office in a farm outhouse.'

By 12 October, the 3rd and 4th Infantry Divisions of II Corps were moving into position on the left of I Corps. The sector for which the BEF was responsible stretched along the border from Maulde northwards to Halluin, protecting the industrial areas of Tourcoing, Roubaix and Lille. A defensive left flank, running north-east to south-west, was formed along the River Lys from Halluin to Armentières, manned by the French 51st Division.

'Great Britain's undertaking,' according to the Official History, 'to have two corps assembled in France thirty-three days after mobilization was fulfilled.' It was a small contribution and certainly a long way short of what the French expected. As Chief of the Imperial General Staff (CIGS), Sir Edmund Ironside, observed in January 1940: 'Our own army is just a little one and we are dependent on the French. We have not even the same fine army we had in 1914. All depends on the French army and we can do nothing about it.'[3]

Senior field commanders were deeply worried about their troops' readiness for war. Shortly after his arrival in France on 29 September 1939, Lieutenant General Alan Brooke, commander of II Corps, expressed his concerns about his formation going straight into the line on the Franco-Belgian border. He felt that his corps was 'at present unfit for war and requires at least one to one and a half months training'. He was assured, however, that the early move of the Corps was a political gesture to the French, and that he would 'be given time to finish training the corps out here'.[4]

Lieutenant General Sir John Dill, commander of I Corps was

equally concerned. Brooke found him 'still very depressed about the general state of unpreparedness for war. We condoled with each other on the lack of equipment and shortage of training of many components.'[5]

Years of defence cuts had rendered the British Army of 1939 a mere shadow of the highly efficient fighting force it had become by the end of the First World War. Lessons had been learned at great cost during those grim years. With peace came the inevitable cutbacks, driven by economic pressures and the nation's desire never to go to war on such a scale again. Within a year of the Armistice, the British Treasury was demanding defence cuts amounting to some 73 per cent – from £502 million to £135 million. Out of this reduced figure, the Royal Air Force and the Army were to share £75 million.

The Cabinet also outlined a plan for future defence spending. It stated:

> It should be assumed that the British Empire will not be engaged in any great war during the next ten years, and that no Expeditionary Force is required for that purpose . . . The principle function of the Military and Air Forces is to provide garrisons for India, Egypt, the new mandated territories (other than self governing) under British control, as well as to provide the necessary support to the civil power.

Successive governments adopted the 'Ten-Year Rule' as it came to be known. Thus each year the assumed decade was moved forward. The Official History stated:

> The services were drastically reduced and for thirteen years deficiencies in equipment of the small forces retained were allowed to accumulate. It was not so with other countries. No general reduction of armaments followed our lead, and in March 1932, the danger of our position was at last admitted, the ten-year rule was abandoned and during the next two years the need for rearmament was discussed (there was little more than discussion) while economic, military and political policies contended for mastery.

Bernard Montgomery, in 1939 a Major General commanding the 3rd Infantry Division, summarized the situation, albeit in hindsight, in his post-war memoirs. He considered that:

> The British Army was totally unfit to fight a first-class war on the continent of Europe. It had for long been considered that in the event of another war with Germany the British contribution to the defence of the West should consist mainly of naval and air forces. How any politician could imagine that, in a world war, Britain could avoid sending her Army to fight alongside the French passes all understanding.
>
> In the years preceding the outbreak of war no large-scale exercises with troops had been held in England for some time. Indeed, the Regular Army was unfit to take part in a realistic exercise.[6]

The decision even to send an Expeditionary Force to France at the outbreak of war had only been taken in February 1939, leaving a lot of lost ground still to be made up. Some of the Army's manpower was spread around the world. Figures for 1938 reveal there were 90,628 men overseas. By far the largest contingent was in India: forty-seven battalions of infantry comprising of 55,498 men. Among them was the 1st Battalion Royal Norfolk Regiment which was nearing the end of a ten-year posting. In the Far East were 12,143 men in eight battalions, while in the West Indies there were 1,800. The Middle East and Mediterranean were garrisoned by eighteen battalions numbering 21,187 men. Those in the Middle East would need to protect the Suez Canal and oil interests. In Britain at the time there were 106,704 men.

Certainly Britain could expect quality reinforcements from the armies of Australia, New Zealand, Canada and South Africa, but all this would take time. Therefore, on the European front only four regular divisions could be immediately committed to France, with a fifth to follow at the end of the year.

Expanding an army that two decades of underfunding had reduced to a 'Cinderella Service' gathered momentum as the Government turned its attention to the Territorials. On 29 March, the Cabinet decided that the strength of the Territorial Army should be doubled with each TA unit duplicating itself; the target, on paper at least, was 340,000 men. This decision, however, appears to have been taken without consulting the professional head of the Army, the Chief of the Imperial General Staff, who at that time was Lord Gort. Gort actually told Montgomery 'that he knew nothing about it until he saw it announced one morning in the Press'.[7]

Just under a month later, a limited form of conscription was introduced under the Military Training Act. By the end of June 200,000 men aged twenty to twenty-one had registered for service.

Major General Pownall, Director of Military Operations and Intelligence, considered that it would take at least another eighteen months 'before this paper Army is an Army in the flesh . . . What an unholy mess our politicians have made of the rebirth of our Army through shortsightedness, unwillingness to face facts and prejudice against the Army.'[8]

Some senior Army figures were no less critical of the Government's choice for Commander-in-Chief of the BEF, General Lord Gort. Montgomery believed that the appointment 'was a mistake; the job was above his ceiling.'[9]

Lieutenant General Brooke felt that Sir John Dill would have been the better choice. 'I do wish,' he wrote on 21 November, 'he was C-in-C instead of Gort, he has twice the vision and ten times the ability. Gort's brain has lately been compared to that of a glorified boy scout! Perhaps unkind, but there is a great deal of truth in it.'[10]

Brooke's assessment of his commander continued in the following day's diary entry. 'Gort is a queer mixture, perfectly charming, very definite personality, full of vitality, energy and joie de vivre, and gifted with great powers of leadership. But he just fails to see the big picture and is continually returning to those trivial details which counted a lot when commanding a battalion, but which should not be the main concern of a Commander-in-Chief.'[11]

Another name linked to the command of the BEF was General Sir Edmund Ironside. According to Montgomery, rumour suggested that the offer had at one stage been made, to compensate for Ironside's being passed over when Gort was appointed CIGS in 1937. In any event, Ironside would not have been acceptable to the Commander-in-Chief of the Allied Armies, General Maurice Gamelin, whose own appointment as supreme commander had been recommended by Gort. But as the BEF assembled in France, Ironside did receive some recompense with his appointment as CIGS.

If his ability to command a formation the size of the BEF was called into question, there could certainly be no questioning the bravery of 54-year-old John Standish Surtees Prendergast Vereker, 6th Viscount Gort. A former Grenadier Guardsman, he had served with great distinction in the First World War. Wounded four times, mentioned in despatches eight times, he was awarded the Military Cross, the Distinguished Service Order and two Bars, and finally, in September 1918, the highest award of all, the Victoria Cross. Little wonder then that Army Public Relations endeavoured to encourage the press to call him 'Tiger' instead of 'Fat Boy', as he was known by the men. Unflattering it may have been but it was not without a certain affection; he was greatly respected, a soldier's soldier. The men knew that to an extent he shared their hardships, shunning the more comfortable life that some officers in his position might enjoy. He even slept on a camp bed. His simple tastes were in stark contrast to the high living of his French counterparts.

Although some may have lacked confidence in Gort's ability to lead the BEF, the C-in-C was in a difficult position for overall command rested with the French. Gort's instructions, signed by the Minister for War, Leslie Hore-Belisha and dated 3 September 1939, made the British Army's role clear:

1. The role of the force under your command is to co-operate with our Allies in the defeat of our common enemy.

2. You will be under the command of the French Commander-in-Chief 'North-East Theatre of Operations'. In the pursuit of the common object you will carry out loyally any instructions issued by him. At the same time, if any order given by him appears to you to imperil the British Field Force, it is agreed between the British and French Governments that you should be at liberty to appeal to the British Government before executing that order. While it is hoped that the need for such an appeal will seldom, if ever, arise you will not hesitate to avail yourself of your right to make it, if you think fit.

3. Initially the force under your command will be limited to two corps of two divisions with G.H.Q., Corps and L. of C. Troops together with a Royal Air Force Component of two bomber, four fighter and six Army co-operation squadrons.

4. It is the desire of His Majesty's Government to keep the British Forces under your command, as far as possible, together. If at any time the French Commander-in-Chief 'North-East Theatre of Operations' finds it essential for any reason to transfer any portion of the British troops to an area other than that in which your main force is operating, it should be distinctly understood that this is only a temporary arrangement, and that as soon as practicable the troops thus detached should be reunited to the main body of the British forces.

Paragraphs 5 and 6 dealt with the Royal Air Force Component and the Advanced Air Striking Force.

Gort's orders, therefore, placed him under the command of General Alphonse Georges, C-in-C 'North-East Theatre of Operations.' The BEF was in Army Group 1 commanded by General Gaston Billotte.

The French tended to look down on Gort as if he were a more junior officer. Perhaps it was a reflection of the small British contribution to the Allied cause. But Gort was a loyal soldier, who accepted that the French generals were his seniors and resolutely accepted the situation, however unsatisfactory.

While German forces mopped up the last vestiges of Polish resistance, Hitler outlined a 'Peace Plan' in a speech in the Reichstag on 6 October. Now that Poland had collapsed, the necessity of war between France, Britain and Germany had been removed. He called for a peace conference, free trade, arms limitations and the return of colonies. He wanted friendship with Britain and had no territorial claims against France. All the Allies had to do was accept the order that now existed in Eastern Europe.

Three days later, and before the Allies had even rejected the proposals, Hitler issued his generals with Führer Directive No. 6. They were to plan an offensive 'through Luxembourg, Belgium and

Holland [which] must be launched at the earliest possible moment'. Further delay:

> will entail the end of Belgium and perhaps Dutch neutrality, to the advantage of the Allies. The purpose of this offensive will be to defeat as much as possible of the French army and of the forces of the Allies fighting on their side, and at the same time to win as much territory as possible in Holland, Belgium and northern France to serve as a base for the successful prosecution of the air and sea war against England and as a wide protection area for the economically vital Ruhr.

Codenamed *Fall Gelb* (Case Yellow), Army High Command, *Oberkommando des Heeres* (OKH), was to work out the detail. But the Commander-in-Chief, General Walther von Brauchitsch and Chief of Staff, General Franz Halder, were reluctant to launch an offensive on the Western Front immediately. They had not yet had time to analyse fully the Army's overall performance in the Polish campaign and thus strengthen any weaknesses that might have become apparent. The French Army was considerably larger than that of Poland and if the campaign dragged on through the remainder of autumn and into winter, troops were liable to become bogged down in deteriorating weather. Hitler, however, had scant regard for the French. The power he feared was Great Britain. While her forces in France were still small, he felt an early strike was necessary. If the BEF of 1939 was anything like that of 1914, then no matter its size, it was liable to punch well above its weight when fighting broke out.

The General Staff remained cautious, developing a plan similar to the Schlieffen Plan used in 1914: an attack through Belgium. *Fall Gelb* was not expected to bring outright victory within a matter of weeks. The objective was to secure air and sea bases in Belgium for operations against Britain, yet Hitler was never enthusiastic about it. Towards the end of October, he suggested an attack through the Ardennes, but as discussions went on only minor modifications were made. In January, a careless breach in security caused a radical rethink.

Allied strategic thinking had been summarized before the outbreak of war:

We should be faced by enemies who would be more fully prepared than ourselves for a war on a national scale, would have superiority in air and land forces, but would be inferior at sea and in general economic strength. In the circumstances, we must be prepared to face a major offensive directed at either France or Britain or against both. To defeat such an offensive we should have to concentrate all our initial efforts and during this time our major strategy would have to be defensive.[12]

British naval superiority enabled an effective blockade to be mounted against Germany. In the meantime, the build-up of manpower and materials would continue at pace. The intention was for the Allies to launch a major offensive in 1941 or 1942, by which time their armed forces would be fully prepared. (On 8 September 1939, the British Government had planned for a three-year war.) Germany, naturally, was liable to attack at any time and when this came it would have to be held. Although the entire length of the Franco-German border was guarded by the Maginot Line, a complex of interconnected fortifications, the frontiers with Luxembourg and Belgium were largely unprotected. There they would have to rely on the strength and determination of the Allied armies, and the defensive positions which could be constructed in the time available. In essence, the Maginot Line would have to be linked to the sea by the defence of some 200 miles of open borders.

The German High Command's reluctance, much to the chagrin of Hitler, to launch an offensive during the autumn and winter, gave the Allies time to improve and deepen the frontier defences. Lord Gort wrote:

When I Corps arrived in its allotted sector an almost contin-uous anti-tank obstacle existed in the form of a ditch covered by concrete blockhouses built to mount anti-tank guns and machine-guns. While defences continued to be developed along the lines of the original plan, based on close defence of the frontier, it was also necessary to organize the position . . . The whole scheme involved the immediate construction of field defences and the duplication of the anti-tank obstacle in the forward zone.

It became known as the Gort Line and the Norfolks' sector at Rumegies was, according to Captain Barclay, 'on the right of the whole British line. In fact, my company was the right-hand company of the British line and I had the French on my right.'

Throughout October and November, the Holy Boys laboured with pick and shovel on the frontier defences.

'We were digging trenches,' Bob Brown explained, 'and helping the Royal Engineers to put up pill-boxes, the concrete pill-boxes, and also doing barbed wire, all along the frontier.'

Progress was hampered by an exceptionally wet autumn: 'Bloody terrible, rain and sleet,' recalled Private Herbert Lines of the Carrier Platoon.

In almost continuous rain, with, as Murray Brown observed, 'only one suit of battle dress available,' they dug, while around them the ground became a sticky, quaking quagmire. New trenches filled with water as quickly as they were dug.

'We tried to go down about six feet,' said Bob Brown 'but if we could manage four and then build the rest above it, that was about our limit.' Pumps were kept going all the while in an attempt to clear the water.

Where no great depth could be achieved revetments had to be constructed. Wattle hurdles were made out of wood and stiffened with lopped off trees or thick stakes and filled with earth and stones.

Photographs of various areas on the Gort Line could easily be mistaken for images taken over twenty years before. Sergeant Walter Gilding of the Mortar Platoon considered the defences to be of the 'First World War pattern'.[13]

As well as contending with adverse weather and ground conditions, the men were also faced with topographical problems. Normally they would endeavour to choose the best sites for defensive positions, but in this instance best practice was sacrificed for a rigid adherence to the line of the frontier. There was little leeway. They had to make use of what natural features there were, which often meant a considerable amount of ingenuity and effort of construction to create a position that offered a good field of fire.

Peter Barclay and his company were told to prepare positions 'bang on the line of this little stream'. It appears to have marked the frontier because they were not able to erect barbed wire on the other side as that was Belgium. In parts the stream provided a good anti-tank obstacle but in other places there was no field of fire for the defenders.

Barclay recalled:

We had to build the most extraordinary positions. Some of my platoon section positions were breast-works and some even were built in trees to raise them off the ground sufficiently to give a field of fire, with, of course, an enormous 'build-up' or foundation underneath . . . Totally impracticable but that was what we were ordered to do. And rather than drop back and take up a reverse slope position, we had to defend the frontier, presumably because this stream did provide in most places an anti-tank obstacle . . .

They were quite extraordinary, these positions and seemingly ridiculous . . . They resembled trenches in trees, though never used in the war at any stage. And I should think people were thankful they didn't have to.

Working under such trying conditions did not spare the BEF from ministerial criticism. On 30 November, the Chief of the Imperial General Staff, Sir Edmund Ironside, told Lieutenant General Brooke that when Hore-Belisha returned to London after visiting the front, 'he informed both the Cabinet and Privy Council that the BEF was doing no work and had left their front unprotected. That we were the laughing stock of the French on either flank and a few similar remarks!'[14]

Both Gort and Ironside, whose own relationship was cool, were united in their dislike of Hore-Belisha. His criticism of the BEF ultimately led to his resignation as Secretary of State for War in January 1940.

Work on the line continued throughout the winter and spring of 1940. By May, 400 concrete pillboxes had been built covering some 40 miles of anti-tank obstacles along the border.

The great irony of the Gort Line was that even in the early stages of its construction, French strategy was turning it into what Sergeant Gilding described as a 'waste of time'. The French knew where they wanted to meet the German offensive – not on French soil but as far forward as possible in Belgium. Belgium, like Holland, was neutral and intended to stay that way, so any reconnaissance of possible forward positions which the Allied armies might need to undertake was forbidden. Britain and France, however, were confident that the German attack would mirror that of 1914 and that their forces would be allowed to cross the frontier once neutrality was violated. They could only hope that the Belgians had taken steps to prepare adequate defensive positions.

With scarcely any military activity on the Western Front apart from training and digging, American journalists dubbed this period the 'Phoney War'. To the British soldiers, it became the 'Bore War'. Boredom was indeed a problem and affected some units worse than others. However, Bob Brown said that there were no crimes or acts of indiscipline in the Battalion. 'We were very easy-going, very free and easy.'

Despite the discomfort and lack of action the Regimental History of the Royal Norfolks said that 'morale remained excellent . . . A few football matches were arranged and concert parties, but lack of accommodation for the latter kept them on a very small scale.' So some of the men from 'A' Company formed their own concert troupe. Barclay remembered that:

> We got out from England mouth organs and flutes and various articles of musical equipment like that, and, supplemented by combs and cheese-paring boards, and things like that, we had a very effective company band. And we used to have concerts about twice a week, and the talent that used to emanate from the company itself was quite remarkable. The soldiers used to enjoy this very much and they were envied much by the other companies in the battalion . . . a lot of guests came to enjoy [the concerts] . . .
>
> We had cross-country runs, we had football; really kept them busy in some way or other absolutely all the time. And morale was extremely high and stayed that way through the winter.

The 'Phoney War' was not without its alarms. The Dutch military attaché in Berlin, Major Gijsbertus Sas, was warned on 5 November of an impending invasion of the Low Countries. He immediately informed the Belgian attaché and the message was passed to the British and French. By 10 November, the BEF, in a high state of readiness, was still awaiting the German advance. Lieutenant General Brooke thought that 'the probability of an early invasion of Belgium or Holland or both seems most likely. All reports point to an early move, but it may well be some form of bluff. The suspense is somewhat trying.'[15]

The suspense continued for several days. On the 12th, information received appeared to make it a certainty that the invasion would commence some time between that day and the 15th. But the Western Front remained quiet and by the 20th, the BEF had reduced its state of readiness.

The dull, back-breaking routine for the men of the BEF was brightened towards the year's end by the visit of King George VI to the front. On 5 December, he reached Rumiges where the Norfolks lined the street in his honour. He left his car and walked down the line of smartly turned out men. Other VIPs who visited the Holy Boys that December were Prime Minister Neville Chamberlain, the Duke of Gloucester and the First Lord of the Admiralty, Winston Churchill.

Barclay reckoned that his company received more visits than any other. They were on the right of the line and 'had these extraordinary tree positions which nobody else had ever seen before. And they were a point of considerable interest and comment, I may say.'

Churchill's visit was fondly remembered by Barclay. 'He was in tremendously good form and he came along followed by an array of brass . . . I had a little mongrel which had come over and joined me from Belgium . . . We were walking along from one position to another and she suddenly started barking at a pile of faggots.'

'A little sport, a little sport,' said Winston, intrigued.

'Yes, if we play it right,' said Barclay.

'Well,' mused Churchill, 'let's play it right. How do you want it played?'

'What we really want to do is get three officers on top of that pile of faggots and have them bounce,' Barclay suggested, 'and then we'll bolt the rabbit and then we'll have a hunt.'

Churchill's eyes lit up, Barclay recalled, 'and the three senior generals were ordered onto this pile of faggots. And directed by Winston, as it were as orchestra conductor, he synchronized the bouncing . . . They had no alternative. I mean, they were just ordered up there by Winston and ordered to bounce. They looked pretty foolish with their ADCs sort of looking on to start with, I must say, but they entered into the spirit of the thing . . . Sure enough, very shortly, the rabbit bolted and we had a most exciting hunt which intrigued Winston no end and slightly confused the generals concerned . . . It was quite a change from the norm.'

Christmas came early for the 2nd Battalion Royal Norfolk Regiment with their celebrations being held on 19 December. Over the festive period itself they would be on the move, heading for the Franco-German border and their first contact with the enemy.

Notes

1. Imperial War Museum, Sound Archive; Herbert Lines' interview, accession number 17297.
2. Lieutenant Colonel C.R. Murray Brown DSO, *Britannia Magazine*, No. 27; reproduced by kind permission of the Trustees of the Royal Norfolk Regimental Museum, Norwich.
3. Macleod, R. and Kelly, Denis (eds), *The Ironside Diaries*, Constable, 1962.
4. Danchev, Alex and Todman, Daniel (eds), *War Diaries 1939–1945: Field Marshal Lord Alanbrooke*, Orion, 2002.
5. *Ibid.*, diary entry for 4 October 1939.
6. Montgomery, Field Marshal Viscount, *Memoirs*, Pen and Sword, 2007, by kind permission of A.P. Watt on behalf of Viscount Montgomery of Alamein.
7. *Ibid.*
8. Bond, Brian (ed.), *Chief of Staff: the Diaries of Lt. Gen. Sir Henry Pownall*, vol I, Leo Cooper, 1972.
9. Montgomery, *Memoirs*.
10. Danchev and Todman, *War Diaries*.
11. *Ibid.*, diary entry for 22 November 1939.
12. Gibbs, N.H., *History of the Second World War: Grand Strategy*, vol. I, HMSO, 1976. Crown Copyright material is reproduced with the permission of the Controller of The Stationery Office and the Queen's Printer for Scotland.
13. Imperial War Museum, Sound Archive; Walter Gilding's interview, accession number 17534.
14. Danchev and Todman, *War Diaries*, entry for 30 November 1939.
15. *Ibid.*, diary entry for 10 November 1939.

CHAPTER 2

'You've done a damned fine show.'

FOUR DAYS AFTER THE ALLIED declaration of war in September 1939, around nine French divisions launched the 'Saar Offensive'. Advancing beyond the Maginot Line, they crossed into German territory encountering little opposition. An excited British press hailed the operation as 'the first big attack on the Siegfried Line' (*Daily Express*), and the 'French Army pouring over the German border' (*Daily Mail*).

For a few minutes each day, the advance was supported, if that is the right word, by 75mm rounds fired from the Hockwald bastion in the Maginot Line. One of the guns actually jammed early on, so artillery support was desultory to say the least. After a penetration of 5 miles on a 16-mile front and the occupation of a few abandoned German villages, General Prételat was ordered by Gamelin to halt on 12 September and take up a 'defensive posture'.

It was a half-hearted gesture towards Poland to set up a diversionary attack; in the words of one French general, 'simply a token invasion'. Readers of the *Daily Express* at the time could be forgiven for believing that it was an outstanding success. A headline on 8 September proclaimed: 'Germany rushes more troops to the West.' But as Poland was overwhelmed, the French Cabinet decided it was time to withdraw Prételat's forces to the Maginot Line.

On the night of 30 September/1 October, the French began a stealthy retreat from the occupied territory. Withdrawal from the advanced position in Warndt and the Saarbrucken Salient was completed by 4 October. On the 16th, the Germans mounted a counter-attack and within forty-eight hours had driven out any remaining covering forces, with few casualties on either side.

After this the frontier zone lapsed into relative quiet with little activity apart from patrolling, digging, watching and waiting. Artillery remained silent. There appeared to be a 'Gentleman's Agreement' between the German and French batteries that neither side would shell opposing villages.

As the only potentially 'active' area of the whole Western Front, the British decided that it would be an ideal sector in which troops could gain experience in hostile conditions. The Germans would only be a few hundred yards away and contact inevitable. Lord Gort arranged with General Georges for individual infantry brigades, in turn, to do a short spell of duty on the Saar front. The first was in place by 4 December. The zone utilized was north-east of Metz and several miles to the left of where the French token effort had taken place.

So it was that on Christmas Eve 1939, the Holy Boys entrained for Metz. Winter held Europe in an icy grip; snow blanketed the countryside and conditions had become treacherous. Hitler's cautious generals had been proven correct. An exceptionally wet autumn had merged into one of the coldest winters since 1889. Temperatures fell so sharply that there were reports of the sea freezing at Boulogne, Dungeness and Folkestone.

With 'C' Company away on leave, Lieutenant Colonel Hayes requested that a company of the 2nd Battalion Dorsetshire Regiment, serving in 5 Brigade, be attached to bring his battalion up to strength. The Dorsets duly supplied a company commanded by Major Goff, 'thus,' according to the Regimental History, 'bringing the two regiments once again into close association and reviving the "Norset" tradition established in the 1914–18 war.'[1]

The rail journey was long and dreary. Ernie Farrow said that there was no heat on the train and they were 'frozen stiff to Metz'. After travelling all night and for the whole of Christmas morning, they pulled into Metz at around 1300.

'And from there,' said Bob Brown, 'we then marched out to evacuated houses for billets overnight.'

Their journey, however, was by no means over. There were still several miles to travel over roads rendered treacherous by snow and ice, before they reached their positions in front of the Maginot Line.

Running parallel to the Franco-German border for just over 87 miles, from the Swiss frontier near Basle to the Luxembourg border near Longwy, the Maginot Line was the Western Front in concrete. It consisted of a chain of subterranean fortresses, linked by underground railways and served by their own power plants. Constructed between 1930 and 1937, it bore the name of André Maginot who was Minister for War when work on the colossal undertaking began. He died three years into the project.

Captain Barclay recalled a visit to one of the forts, probably Fort Hackenburg, which was in the sector:

> It was absolutely unbelievable. It was controlled like the hub of a battleship. There was an enormous office with press buttons and switches all over the place, deep down in the bowels of one of these forts. And when a mortar, for instance, was called upon to fire, a button was pressed and a cupola on top of a tower rose up. And this thing fired, and then having fired it was lowered down again.
>
> All these guns and weapons that the Maginot Line was equipped with had specific areas to fire on to. The territory in front of the line, including and beyond the ditches and barbed wire entanglements, were chequered out in squares and certain weapons were designed to bring fire to bear on partic-ular squares. The commander within that particular sector of the Maginot Line lived in this control room and, according to what the observation posts reported, he brought fire to bear on any particular sector that was required.
>
> It was a most extraordinary, complicated and fascinating arrangement. There were little railway lines running all over the place. The heavy shells weren't manhandled at all. They were run in on pulleys and fed into the breeches of the guns. It was mechanized to the nth degree.
>
> And it went down to tremendous depths too, as far as the tunnels and operations rooms were concerned.

It also made the French complacent, confident that the great line was impregnable, as Barclay explained:

> They had a motto, '*On ne passé pas*', which applied basically to the Maginot Line and the inhabitants of the Maginot Line. All the French soldiers and a lot of the French population had

little badges with a fortress and *On ne passé pas* stamped across it. This had an adverse effect, in fact, on the French Army as a whole. They had a totally passive attitude to the war; an indoctrination of being ready to receive rather than go on the offensive. They were firmly of the opinion that the Maginot Line couldn't be crossed anywhere and that as long as they sat on that and used the enormous fire power it was capable of producing, they could keep the Germans on the other side.

They were dead against any form of patrolling even in this position way in front of the Maginot Line. They just sat in their trenches all through the night and waited for anything to happen that might happen. I think the Germans probably appreciated that they could approach the sector on our left which was where the French army forces were with impunity rather than our sector. They were totally unoffensive-minded [sic]; this was a very sad state of affairs in fact.

French complacency was not lost on the Germans, playing right into their hands during the initial stages of the war. Protecting the German borders was the West Wall or Siegfried Line, and it was not such a formidable barrier.

Major General F.W. von Mellenthin wrote in *Panzer Battles*:

I soon realized what a gamble the Polish Campaign had been, and the grave risks which were run by our High Command. The second-class troops holding the Wall were badly equipped and inadequately trained, and the defences were far from being impregnable fortifications pictured by our propaganda. Concrete protection of more than three feet was rare, and as a whole the positions were by no means proof against heavy calibre shelling. Few of the strongpoints were sited to fire in enfilade and most of them could have been shot to pieces by direct fire, without the slightest risk to the attackers. The West Wall had been built in such a hurry that many of the positions were sited on forward slopes. The anti-tank obstacles were of trivial significance, and the more I looked at the defences the less I could understand the completely passive attitude of the French.

Apart from sending some local patrols into the outlying areas (very 'outlying') of Saarbrücken, the French had kept very quiet and left the West Wall alone. This negative attitude was bound to affect the fighting morale of their troops, and was calculated to do much more harm than our propaganda, effective though it was.[2]

Seven years of labour and over 7,000 million francs had been sunk into the Maginot Line, creating a static defence system that the German Army would initially by-pass. French military planners knew it and fully expected the main German thrust to come through Belgium. Hitler would not respect Belgian neutrality in his desire for a final reckoning with France; as he had said in *Mein Kampf*, 'one last decisive battle'.

Lieutenant General Alan Brooke was also not convinced that the Maginot Line was such a marvellous military accomplishment. 'Millions of money stuck in the ground for purely static defence,' he wrote in his diary in February 1940 after a visit to Fort Hackenburg, 'and the total firepower developed by these works bears no relation to the time, work and money spent in their construction.'[3]

Major General von Mellenthin also noted: 'that many of the French strongpoints were not proof against shells or bombs, and moreover, a large number of positions had not been sited for all-round defence and were easy to attack from the blind side with grenades and flame-throwers.'[4]

'It extends to the sea,' was the typical Gallic response to the question where does the Maginot Line end? But those men who had dug through clinging mud on the Gort Line knew otherwise.

Forming part of the overall defence system of the Maginot Line were support lines, the number depending on the sector. In the British brigade area there were three: the *ligne de contact*, the front line, as its name implies in contact with the enemy; the *ligne de receuil*, a recoil or lay-back position; then came the Maginot Line itself, and the *ligne d'arrêt*, the final stop line, intended as a line of last stand should the enemy penetrate the fortress area. During a brigade's tour of duty each battalion occupied one of these lines in turn.

The journey from Metz took the Holy Boys five days. Travelling under cover of darkness for concealment, progress was slowed by the atrocious weather conditions. Temperatures falling as low as -24°C created hazardous road conditions and even froze the anti-freeze mixture in the radiators of the transport. Walter Gilding said that it was so cold that they found ice inside the tins of corned beef. For internal warmth, the men enjoyed hot cocoa with a rum ration.

As a dispatch rider, Albert Pooley found his job exacting during the bitter weather. With French roads little better than skating rinks, most of his journeys by motorcycle were made feet down for stability, but he loved riding and enjoyed the work immensely.

Unfortunately, one trip, which took him to the River Moselle to deliver dispatches to the Transport Officer, cost him dearly. On the way back he met a friend and while chatting began to feel dizzy. He took a medicinal drink to try and warm himself and then slept for a while. When he awoke he realized that time was against him and he would be back very late. Still feeling unwell, he pressed on but the symptoms grew worse and he was eventually forced to seek refuge in a railway station.

The stationmaster appears to have been an officious man and totally unsympathetic to Pooley's plight. As soon as a British vehicle came along the road, the official waved it down and reported the presence of his unwanted guest. Unluckily for Pooley, beside the vehicle's driver sat the battalion's Motor Transport Officer. Pooley and his brand-new and undamaged BSA motorcycle, which actually belonged to the Signals Sergeant, were bundled into the truck. Both driver and officer were convinced that the dispatch rider had been drinking and took him straight to the guardroom at Kedange. Pooley's request to see the Medical Officer was ignored and he was charged with being 'Drunk and incapable whilst in charge of a military vehicle, whilst carrying dispatches in the face of the enemy'.

Found guilty, Albert Pooley's ten years as a signaller were brought to an end. Lieutenant Colonel Hayes sentenced him to a forfeiture of pay and a return to ordinary front-line duties with 'A' Company. What was never taken into consideration was that Pooley's illness was the annual recurrence of the malaria he had contracted while serving with the regiment in India.[5]

As the New Year of 1940 dawned, the Holy Boys were in

position in the *ligne de contact*, where between 800 and 1,000 yards separated them from the German lines. The heavy snow had turned the rolling landscape of open valleys and wooded ridges into a sterile white wilderness several inches deep. Isolated farmsteads and villages were lifeless shells, as though some foul pestilence had passed through the land. The French military had moved the inhabitants away to safety, sometimes in such great haste that it was almost as if they had simply popped out for a few moments. Belongings, apart from those that could be easily carried, had been abandoned, left to the mercy of looters. Khaki-clad figures brought life back to some of the deserted homesteads behind the forward positions when headquarters were established. The Norfolks made their HQ in the village of Waldweistroff about a mile behind the line.

'The front occupied was very wide,' says the Regimental History, 'and held by a series of defended platoon positions in small woods and copses, the gaps between them being anything up to half a mile.'

Three companies were deployed forward with Major Goff's company of Dorsets in reserve. Captain Barclay's 'A' Company was on the left of the line, the centre was held by 'B' Company under Captain Allen, while 'D' Company, commanded by Captain Richardson, was on the right.

Bob Brown was a signaller with 17 Platoon of 'D' Company. He said that they were situated 'in very small dug-outs in front of a wood' on the side of a valley. The German positions were about 2 or 3 miles away facing them on the opposite side of the valley.

Apart from trenches and wire there were few other signs that this was an active war zone. Ernie Farrow recalled:

There was hardly anything above ground – only snow. There were trenches that had been dug down and revetted with duckboards in them. They were all dry because of these frosts which dried everything up. In some places they were dug underground. The company headquarters was underground, but we were on top in the trenches . . . It was very, very cold and at night-time we got inside our big bags. During the day we managed to find some sandbags that we filled full of straw and wrapped them round our legs to keep our legs and feet warm, much better to walk about like that as well.

Even though the ground was dry, it was so hard that when it came to improving the positions or digging fresh trenches, Barclay remembered using explosives in the form of hand grenades to blow holes in the frozen earth.

When the Mortar Platoon took over their position from the Royal Scots, the mortar's base plate was solidly frozen into the ground, so Sergeant Gilding handed his over to the Scots.

'When I was relieved,' he explained, 'I did the same thing. You just couldn't dig it out.'

The mortar pit itself had been dug into a railway embankment. Nearby a small shelter had also been dug with the added comfort of 'a little fire stove place . . . with a metal funnel coming out of the top'. The Platoon lit the stove only to find that their shelter became very smoky. For their five-day tour of duty, the Platoon put up with the smoke until the last day, when it was discovered that as a joke the Scots had stuffed a pair of socks into the chimney.

At first their routine differed little from that of the Gort Line – the positions needed improving. The Army had trained Ernie Farrow in carpentry and he found his skills very much in demand by all the companies in building bunkers and making trench supports.[6] Lorry loads of Dannet wire were brought up which had to be positioned at night. And while they worked, the men knew they had to be vigilant and keep their heads down, otherwise they could easily fall prey to snipers.

Across no man's land ran a railway embankment, on which were parked some carriages. Through his field glasses, Peter Barclay watched German soldiers moving about in the carriages. It was obvious to him that they were being used as an observation post and he thought it would make a jolly good gunner target.

'So I ordered fire to be brought down by the French artillery 75s which were supporting us,' he said, 'and nothing happened, to my indignation. I got on to Battalion Headquarters to find out why I wasn't receiving the response to which I reckoned I was entitled.'

'"Oh, it's not a legitimate target," was HQ's response. "The only legitimate target you should know by now is a working party in the open."

'And that was the only target, such was the Phoney War, that we were entitled to shoot at. So we never shot at these Germans.'

Walter Gilding, too, found it frustrating that the Mortar Platoon could not bombard the Germans who were about 900 yards away.

'Each morning,' he said, 'they used to come out with a towel round their necks, where they'd been having a wash, and wave at us.' They were certainly in range but the Platoon was 'ordered not to fire by Battalion Headquarters, by the CO. At the time we thought maybe they're discussing peace terms or something of that nature and they didn't want us to provoke the situation. It didn't make sense to us. We were there to fight a war and we weren't allowed to get on with it.'

While they sat huddled in their smoky outpost, Gilding noticed a dog run across their front. Later, he saw French soldiers dragging the reluctant creature back whence it came. This happened again and again until Gilding discovered that the animal was going between two French outposts spaced well apart. As there was no communication between the two posts, the dog, in its headlong dash, was carrying messages to what it considered to be a friendly post where it was well fed and treated kindly. In the other post it was deprived of food and ill-treated. When a message needed to be sent, the dog was released and naturally made straight for food and fuss only to be dragged back to purgatory later.

German patrols scoured no man's land during those long winter nights. Sometimes they passed through the widespread forward positions but no clashes occurred. British patrolling was less frequent, although Captain Barclay laid great store by them.

'It's frightfully good training for one thing,' he said, 'and its very good for morale to feel that you're being offensive rather than sitting on your backside and letting them come sort of thing. And always, I insisted in whatever stage of command I had that patrolling was carried out.'

Evidently, Barclay also wanted to draw the Germans out, to elicit some form of response from them. 'We went down to a tiny little village near Waldwisse [and] rang the church bells. This created the most incredible consternation among the French more than anybody else.' They then hung around waiting to see if anybody came to investigate 'but no luck'.

Two separate patrols carried out by the Norfolks during the night of 3/4 January were successful and provided notable firsts not only for the Battalion but also for the BEF.

According to the Regimental History, a patrol consisting of three men led by Lieutenant Patrick Everitt 'penetrated through the enemy front and across the border into Germany, being the first time a British patrol had actually crossed the frontier during the war. It returned without being brought to action and with much valuable information. Lieutenant Everitt and his patrol received the congratulations of the Brigadier on their achievement.'

Both the patrols faced the additional hazard of a night of broken cloud: bright moonlight at one moment and pitch darkness the next. During the clear spells, the moon's light reflecting off the deep snow created that pale, almost ethereal, twilight in which figures and objects can be clearly defined.

Peter Barclay led the other patrol consisting of his company's Second in Command, Second Lieutenant Murray Brown, Lance Corporal H.M. Davis and two others. They were hand-picked men.

'You've got to pick a chap who goes on patrol very carefully,' Barclay explained, 'reliable, not flusterable,[sic] and intelligent, reasonably intelligent in case he got cut off and had to get back on his own.'

Their orders were to gather intelligence on the German positions behind an elaborate barbed-wire entanglement in front of the railway station at the village of Waldwisse. A prisoner was also wanted for identification purposes.

It took the patrol about an hour and a half to reach the German line but the first positions they came to were deserted. Tracks in the snow led them through yards and yards of wire, but they were forced to stop occasionally and do some cutting. They moved deep into enemy territory and gathered much valuable information regarding the enemy dispositions. But Barclay still wanted a prisoner and so far they had not encountered any Germans. Then they came across a house which appeared to be occupied.

'We knew they were either in there or recently in there,' Barclay recalled during an interview for the *Eastern Daily Press* in 1992. 'There were boot prints in the snow and smoke coming out of the chimney.'

Leaving Second Lieutenant Murray Brown to organize cover from a railway embankment, Barclay and Lance Corporal Davis went to investigate.

We crept in, went down to the lower floor into a basement room. There was a glowing fire but there weren't any bloody Germans there. And then I saw this lovely carved wooden bear being used as a doorstopper and I thought I'll jolly well take that home when suddenly there was this frightful explosion and I fell on my face.

A grenade [a light egg – Bakelite – grenade] had landed between my legs, made rather a nasty mess of my boots but hadn't affected me in any other way at all.

Then, of course, there was absolutely all hell let loose. Up went the Very lights; German fire from absolutely point-blank range all round us and I couldn't get my prisoner. In fact, we had a hell of a job to get out.

The official statement, as quoted by a Special Correspondent with the BEF and published in the *Eastern Daily Press* on 13 January 1940 said:

The patrol replied vigorously and took cover in a neigh-bouring ditch but in doing so lost touch with the other officer of the patrol.

Captain Barclay endeavoured to get into touch with the other officer without result.

The enemy having started to work round his flanks and Captain Barclay having exhausted his bombs, withdrew his patrol without loss in spite of enemy bombing and small arms fire at close range.

The patrol reached our lines some 1200 yards away safely.

Second Lieutenant Murray Brown, however, had been left behind. They had agreed a rendezvous point on the German side of the barbed-wire entanglement where they would wait for ten minutes for anyone who became separated from the main party. Murray Brown had failed to appear but managed to get back on his own. Barclay recalled:

He didn't know the sector quite as well as I did, and he came back, in fact, not in front of our positions but in front of the French positions. He had a terrible time getting in. He shouted out who he was but they were fully prepared to sort of shoot at anything that moved on sight and ask questions afterwards. So he did have a bit of a problem making it. Anyhow, he arrived in the morning safe and sound, to my great relief.

According to his newspaper interview of 1992, when Barclay reported to Lieutenant Colonel Hayes he got 'a blistering rocket' for having taken his company Second in Command without the CO's authority.

The next day Brigadier Warren came to the Norfolks' sector. He was 'frightfully pleased' continued Barclay, 'and patted me on the back and said: "You've done a damned fine show. It's the best bit of news that's happened to the BEF since we came out here."

'There was my colonel listening and the French general commanding the artillery was in the party too. He said: "Mon brave capitaine! Mon brave capitaine!" and embraced me on both cheeks. My colonel said: "If you don't deserve a decoration for anything else, you do for the way you accepted those embraces."'

The Holy Boys' spell on the front line came to an end on 5 January. Under cover of darkness, they moved back to the *ligne de receuil* where they spent the remainder of the night in billets at Monneren. The Battalion's Carrier Platoon, however, commanded by Lieutenant Everitt, remained at the front to form part of the Brigade's 'patrol team'.

During daylight on Sunday, 7 January, Everitt led a patrol over the crest of a hill which brought them within sight of a German position. Determined to get even closer to this enemy defensive post, Everitt hurried on, opening a considerable gap between himself and his men. Suddenly, German machine-guns opened fire, sweeping across the whole area and pinning the patrol to the ground. Everitt was hit, but because he was so far ahead and the German fire was so intense, nobody was able to reach him.

After dark, patrols were sent out to search for him but returned without success. Enemy wireless broadcasts subsequently revealed the young Lieutenant's fate. Gravely injured, he had been taken to a German hospital where he died from his wounds two days later. The Germans buried him with full military honours. Son of Sir Clement and Lady Everitt, he was the first officer of the BEF to be killed in action.

On 13 January, the Battalion received orders to return to Rumiges. Three days later they left the hutted camp at Kedange, which had been built amongst the trees in a large wood just to the rear of the Maginot Line, and headed for the railway at Metz. Winter had not eased its Arctic grasp, temperatures were still extremely low and road conditions treacherous. After a rail journey lasting thirty hours they reached Rosult from where they marched to Rumiges.

News of their exploits on the Saar front had already reached the British public. In an editorial published on Saturday, 13 January 1940, the *Eastern Daily Press* said:

The greatest honour has fallen to the Royal Norfolk Regiment in providing the first two British soldiers to receive decorations for bravery in the field in this war. For his conspicuous gallantry, coolness and resource Captain F.P. Barclay has received from Lord Gort the Military Cross, and Lance Corporal H. Davis, who shared his hazardous adventure, has been awarded the Military Medal. The circumstances in which they won their decorations were dangerous in the extreme. Captain Barclay had taken a patrol far behind the German lines, and in their quest for information and prisoners they searched a house in the cellars of which enemy soldiers were hiding. Later they were attacked with grenades and rifle fire and though they became separated from the rest of their patrol they managed to return to their lines unhurt. Norfolk, no less than the regiment whose proud traditions they have so splendidly upheld, will be proud of these men and congratulate them on their honour and escape. This is the first mention that has been made of the Royal Norfolk Regiment in France since the war began. It could not have been made in finer terms.

The remainder of the patrol was mentioned in dispatches.

For the media in general here was a real war story, one that would help maintain the nation's morale. The Government's policy towards the press had been somewhat confusing with war reporting being given a low priority. Good news stories were what they wanted the people to read. Guidelines drawn up in September

1939 by the Ministry of Information, Press and Censorship Division said that French and English newspapers, particularly the French, must be filled 'with fraternization stories and human interest stories about the English in France. Only in that way will the awkward period [of the Phoney War] be covered.'

The Holy Boys had struck the right note. The BEF had a band of heroes who had taken on the Germans in their own backyard and come through unscathed, apart from Barclay's boots. Reporters, photographers and newsreel cameramen descended on the Norfolks. For the benefit of one cameraman, Captain Barclay and the members of his patrol recreated the sequence of events. Although staged in daylight, the snow-covered ground gave the black-and-white images captured forever on film a touch of authenticity.

'The rum issue before the patrol set out was of intense interest to the cameraman,' wrote Murray Brown, 'and had to be re-enacted until he was quite satisfied as to its efficiency, a proceeding more than satisfying to the patrol!'

The Holy Boys had also set a benchmark for those units subsequently posted to the forward positions on the Saar front. Lieutenant Halliday of 2nd Battalion Hampshire Regiment described the atmosphere amongst the officers of the 1st Guards Brigade while planning their nightly patrols across no man's land:

> Brigadier 'Becky' [M.B. Beckwith-Smith] appeared each morning to finalize plans for the fighting patrols that night. There was a curiously pot-hunting atmosphere. The 2nd Battalion Royal Norfolk Regiment had been there just before us and their Fighting Patrol, led by Peter Barclay, had surprised a German patrol and captured a prisoner. Peter was given the Military Cross for his exploits and our patrol commanders obviously reckoned they were in the running for another one.[7]

Barclay, of course, had not taken a prisoner but in the context of the 'Phoney War' the action at Waldwisse caused quite a stir and was naturally prone to exaggeration.

Notes

1. This association with the Dorsets arose during the terrible and costly campaign in Mesopotamia, today Iraq, during the First World War. The Battle of Cetsiphon in November 1915 and the subsequent siege of Kut-al-Amara at the turn of the year, had so decimated the forces that recovered wounded and drafts from 2nd Norfolks and 2nd Dorsets were only sufficient to create a combined battalion known as the 'Norsets'.
2. Mellenthin, Major General F.W. von, *Panzer Battles*, Tempus, 2000, reproduced by kind permission of The History Press.
3. Alanbrooke, *War Diaries*, entry for 6 February 1940.
4. Mellenthin, *Panzer Battles*.
5. Jolly, Cyril, *The Vengeance of Private Pooley*, Heinemann, 1956.
6. Jolly, Cyril, *The Man who Missed the Massacre*, self-published by the author, 1986.
7. Sarkar, Dilip, *Guards VC Blitzkrieg 1940*, Ramrod Publications, 1999.

CHAPTER 3

'That is what I call a guard.'

ON WEDNESDAY, 10 JANUARY 1940, a Me 108 took off from an aerodrome near Münster bound for Cologne. The pilot, Major Hoenmanns, was flying an old friend Hellmuth Reinberger, a major in the paratroopers, to a secret conference at German Second Air Fleet Headquarters. Considering the highly sensitive documents that Reinberger was carrying, he should have made the 80-mile journey by rail. However, the two men had enjoyed several drinks the previous evening and when Hoenmanns offered to fly his friend to Cologne, Reinberger agreed, provided the weather was good.

The day dawned fine and the aeroplane climbed into a clear blue winter sky, but never reached Cologne. During the flight, the weather closed in and fog reduced visibility causing Hoenmanns to stray into Belgian air space. Realizing his error, he altered course to head east, but his engine failed and Hoenmanns was forced to crash-land in a field near Mass Mechelen close to the border of Belgium and Holland.

The documents in Reinberger's briefcase contained operational instructions for units subordinate to the Second Air Fleet, which were to take part in the offensive the German Army was to carry out across Belgium, from the Moselle to the North Sea: *Fall Gelb*. Before he had time to destroy all the papers by trying to burn them while concealed behind a hedge, Belgian troops arrived. They were taken to a gendarmerie post where Reinberger made a further attempt to destroy the plans by pushing them into a stove. He was thwarted by a Belgian Army captain and enough papers were retrieved to confirm that the Allies were correct about the projected German offensive.

Gamelin immediately ordered a general alert. Other commanders, however, were sceptical about an imminent attack, especially while the weather remained so hostile. There was also an air of 'cry wolf' about it. *Fall Gelb* had already been postponed several times and sources within Germany itself had informed the Allies accordingly. Shortly before the crash at Mass Mechelen there had been warnings of an impending attack being launched on 17 January.

During a conference at the British GHQ on 12 January, senior officers discussed the possibility of the captured documents being a plant. They felt it unlikely that two German officers would stray accidentally into Belgium carrying such vital documents.

On 14 January, Lieutenant General Brooke wrote:

It seems probable that the whole affair was staged with the object of trying to induce Belgium to call on France and England for military support in the face of such a threat, and thus to provide Germany with an excuse for violating the frontier of Belgium and Holland. We may or may not have been right and so as to leave nothing to chance we are now at 4 hours notice to move. Within the next 24 hours or so we might be able to know how serious the threat is.[1]

Tension eased within those twenty-four hours. The next day Brooke was informed by GHQ that 'a German invasion of Belgium no longer seemed imminent and that yesterday's scare was as we had thought a plant on the part of Germany.'[2]

Plant or not, Hitler was outraged. He dismissed the commander of the Second Air Fleet and replaced him with an officer who was to prove one of Germany's ablest generals, Albert Kesselring. With his long-awaited offensive seriously compromised, the Führer ordered the development of a new plan 'founded on secrecy and surprise'.

General Gamelin had worked on his plans to counter the German thrust through Belgium and Holland throughout the previous autumn, and intended to commit his best forces, including the BEF, to this end. As has already been stated, he wanted to avoid fighting on French soil and meet the *Wehrmacht* as far forward as possible. But this meant his forces leaving the frontier defences along the Franco-Belgian border and increasing the chances of an encounter battle in the open – the kind of battle Gamelin least wanted. His preferred option was to meet the offensive from well-prepared defensive positions, but Belgium's adherence to neutrality was a major stumbling block. The Allies were forbidden to cross the border to reconnoitre any areas they might have to defend. Even then, creating adequate defensive positions would take time. If the Belgians themselves were building defences then all well and good, Gamelin was prepared to take that chance. He remained confident, however, that when the offensive was launched, the British and French would be asked to cross the border to assist, and so he built both Holland and Belgium into his plans.

In Belgium there were three possible defence lines, each using watercourses as a natural obstacle. The first would entail an advance right across the country to take up position along the Albert Canal. Because of the distance involved, the Allied armies would have to be in position well before the assault began. It relied heavily, too heavily, on the Belgian Government abandoning its neutrality at an early stage, giving adequate time for the British and French to reach the canal.

The second option involved a much shorter advance to the River Schelde, known to the French as the River Escaut. This went through two stages of development as explained by Lord Gort:

> The first alternative was to occupy the frontier defences, pushing forward mobile troops to the line of the Escaut, while the French 7th Army were to delay the enemy on the line of the Messines [Mesen] Ridge and Yser [Ijzer] Canal. This plan was soon discarded in favour of the second alternative which was to secure and hold the line of the Escaut itself, from the point at which it crosses the frontier at Maulde northwards to the neighbourhood of Ghent where it was intended to effect a junction with the Belgian forces.

The third main option was an advance of over 60 miles across Belgium to positions east of Brussels along the River Dyle [Dijle], forming a line Antwerp, Louvain [Leuven], Wavre [Waver] and Namur [Namen]. Between Wavre, where the Dyle ceases to be of value as an obstacle, and Namur on the River Meuse, were some 25 miles of open countryside offering very few natural defensive positions. It was known as the Gembloux Gap after the town roughly at its centre. This sector was to be the responsibility of the French First Army under General Blanchard and would lie directly on the right of the BEF's frontage which was to run some 15 miles from Louvain to Wavre.

From mid-November, two operations were being worked out by Allied commanders and their staffs: the advance to the Escaut, Plan E, and the advance to the Dyle, Plan D. Lord Gort wrote:

> The Escaut plan was by far the simpler of the two. It involved sending armoured car reconnaissances to the River Dendre [Dender] to be relieved by divisional cavalry who were later, if necessary, to fight a delaying action backwards to the Escaut; demolitions were provided on both rivers; for the remainder of the force, however, the advance appeared likely to be an easy one, well within a day's march on foot. The Dyle plan, on the other hand, involved an advance of some sixty miles, carried out at a time when every movement was of value over roads not previously reconnoitred, perhaps crowded with refugees moving counter to the Allied armies. Much, too, depended on the resistance with which the Belgians, and perhaps the Dutch, were able to offer the enemy, which at such a time would certainly be making every effort to pierce the line of the Meuse and Albert Canal.

From a military point of view, Gort considered the Dyle option to be the better one. The line itself 'was shorter, it afforded greater depth and its northern portion was inundated. In addition, it represented smaller enemy occupation of Belgian territory.'

General Gamelin initially favoured Plan E, but when information was received that the Belgians were fortifying the Gembloux Gap, he was encouraged to adopt the Dyle option. Nevertheless, work continued on what was to be the final stop line along the Franco-Belgian border.

Shortly after returning from the Saar front, the Holy Boys left Rumegies for billets in nearby Orchies. With their Battalion Commander, Lieutenant Colonel Hayes, posted to the UK on 20 January, to become commandant of a training school at Sheerness,

Major Prattley assumed temporary command until the arrival of Lieutenant Colonel Gerald de Wilton.

Throughout February, the Norfolks remained at Orchies, preparing a new defensive line covering the town itself which gave greater depth to the Gort Line. Walter Gilding spoke of doing 'blockhouse duties' at this time. The Royal Engineers had been building these blockhouses, using local labour, to form a continuous line along the border. He said that they were about 400 yards apart with trenches between. Each blockhouse had a slit in it for a machine-gun or Bren gun and was usually manned by a sergeant and a section of men for a period of duty lasting from three to five days.

During the first week in March, a brigade exercise was carried out, after which they moved to Rubempré, a few miles north of Amiens, for ten days of battalion training in the Doullens training area. At Rubempré, the men found conditions comfortable. They were billeted in cottages and found time to fraternize with the local people. On 18 March, they returned to Orchies.

Bob Brown thought that Orchies was quite a good town. 'There was actually a cinema there with British films, changed every day, so we were in the lap of luxury.'

'Training during the months of February to May,' Murray Brown explained, 'was mainly devoted to anti-parachute exercises, digging and later practising embussing, debussing and night convoy driving with the new differential tail light.'

Peter Barclay said that as they were in a reserve locality, it meant the Battalion had more opportunity to train in other aspects of warfare, such as weapon training to improve marksmanship.

> We spent a certain amount of time on embussing and moving in the dark without lights which was a fairly complicated business. But the soldiers were marvellous and the drivers were to be highly commended.
>
> I remember the first exercise we did which took the whole night and it was pitch dark. We had only one minor casualty, a vehicle skidded off the road into a ditch.

Barclay also recalled a form of roadside lighting produced by the French. It consisted of two tiny lamps which reflected onto the road surface and supposedly could not be seen from above. Also, by setting their lights under the vehicle's radiator, just enough light could be cast on the road in front.

> We also did tactical exercises without troops for the officers and NCOs. But the most important of all is the sub-unit exercise. There's a well-known military adage that if a battalion had well-trained platoons, it's a good battalion. And if platoons were capable of good patrolling exercises and good techniques in the various aspects of warfare, by and large, you are likely to have a good battalion. So there was a major emphasis placed on the training of the section, particularly the platoon and the company as well as the larger formation.

By the spring, the Norfolks' officers were aware of Plan D. The 4th Infantry Brigade of Royal Scots, Royal Norfolks and Lancashire Fusiliers would be on the extreme right of the BEF, forming the junction with the French First Army.

Lord Gort 'judged the time factor to be of paramount importance'. Timing, of course, was critical. The Allies knew that when the offensive came it would be a ferocious all-arms attack with tank concentrations forming the armoured spearheads supported by aircraft. It had served them well in Poland and led to Western newsmen coining the word 'blitzkrieg', literally 'lightning war'. How long the Belgian forward defences could delay such a strike was a matter of chance. The British decided that their advance to the Dyle would have to be carried out non-stop, night and day, unlike the French who favoured a night advance. Gort was therefore prepared to risk attack from the air during daylight hours.

Fortunately, the one truly modern aspect of the British Army at the time was full mechanization, insofar as transporting troops, supplies and equipment were concerned. But even this was compromised by shortages which had been made up by requisitioning civilian vans and lorries. The names of the organizations to which they originally belonged disappeared beneath khaki paint to turn them into military-looking vehicles. Major General Montgomery was scathing about their use. He claimed that much of his transport was 'in bad repair and, when my division moved from the ports up to its concentration area near the French frontier, the countryside of France was strewn with broken-down vehicles'.[3] Overall, however, it was a mobile army and Gort was, therefore, able to allot his 'troop-carrying companies . . . in such a way to complete the move in ninety hours'. But the entire advance would have to be carried out over unfamiliar roads to defensive positions unseen and unprepared by the soldiers who were to man them.

This last problem was solved to some extent by British officers bending the rules by entering neutral Belgium posing as civilians. Captain Barclay and some of his fellow officers in the Battalion had 'mufti' (civilian suits) sent over from England and set off in cars to their sector of the River Dyle which was just north of Wavre.

'And there on the ground,' Barclay explained, 'we reconnoitred the positions we were to take in the event of the Germans attacking from that angle . . . We knew exactly where to go and what positions to dig as soon as we arrived there.'

In March, General Gamelin modified Plan D by placing additional forces on the extreme left of the Allied line. It was to have dire consequences for the campaign as a whole. Able to field some of the most mobile units available to France, General Giraud's Seventh Army was to advance rapidly across Belgium to Breda in Holland, there to link up with the Dutch forces in order to secure the Schelde Estuary. This meant the removal of seven divisions from central reserve.

General Georges had not been comfortable with Plan D right from the outset, but he saw the obvious danger of committing reserve divisions to the far left. If the German offensive through Holland and Belgium proved to be a feint then the Allies were being deprived of an effective means of counter-attack should the main thrust come elsewhere. His concerns were shared by both Billotte and Giraud.

The intended Allied line was now assuming its final shape. The First Army Group would run from Breda in a great arc through Belgium and France to the beginning of the Maginot Line. Commander of this group was General Billotte and the breakdown was a follows: General Giraud's Seventh Army to advance to Breda; sector of the Dyle, Antwerp to Louvain, to be covered by the Belgian Army which would withdraw to this position when unable to hold the Germans on the Albert Canal any longer; from Louvain to Wavre, the BEF; the Gembloux Gap from Wavre to

Namur to be defended by General Blanchard's First Army; General Corap's Ninth Army to advance to positions on the River Meuse from Namur to a point north of Sedan; and General Huntziger's Second Army to remain in position on the Meuse forming junction with the Ninth Army north of Sedan to the Maginot Line.

From there onwards the Second and Third Army Groups would operate behind the Maginot Line and in Alsace-Lorraine. The Alps and the Italian border were covered by the Fourth Army Group.

The BEF had grown during the 'Phoney War' from its original four divisions – by the end of the year a fifth regular division was in place. January 1940 saw the arrival of the first of the Territorial Divisions, the 48th (South Midland); the following month two more arrived: the 50th (Northumbrian) and the 51st (Highland). In April came the 42nd (East Lancashire) and 44th (Home Counties) divisions.

January had also seen the arrival of another unit of Holy Boys, the 7th Battalion – Territorials trained in pioneering duties. Initially, they were GHQ troops but in March it was understood that they had been selected for deployment with the 5th Division to Finland which was at war with Russia. When this war ended on 13 March, 7th Norfolks remained in France, eventually becoming attached to the 51st (Highland) Division.

Another connection with the county of Norfolk was the 65th Anti-Tank Regiment which arrived as part of the 50th (Northumbrian) Division. This was actually the Norfolk Yeomanry whose batteries came from Norwich, Wymondham, Swaffham (Regimental HQ) and King's Lynn. The Regiment dated from 1901, when Edward VII made it known that he wished a regiment of Yeomanry to be raised in Norfolk, of which he would be Honorary Colonel. The Regiment's first commanding officer had been Major H.A. Barclay, uncle of Captain Peter Barclay.

In all, there were ten complete infantry divisions numbering around 237,000 men when hostilities finally broke out in May, plus a further 150,000 supporting troops in France carrying out medical and lines of communications duties.

As far as BEF armoured units were concerned, there was, according to Montgomery: 'somewhere in France, under GHQ, one Army Tank Brigade. For myself, I never saw any of its tanks during the winter or during the active operations in May. And we were the nation which had invented the tank and were the first to use it in battle, in 1916.'[4]

The 1st Armoured Division was in the process of being formed and due to arrive in May. When it did reach France it was too late to help the main body of the BEF.

Seven months had passed and apart from skirmishing on the Saar sector all remained quiet on the Western Front. One newspaperman came up with yet another word to describe this period: 'Sitzkrieg'.

There were those amongst the Allies who wondered if the Germans were going to attack at all. The War Office in London viewed the front as a stalemate. Neville Chamberlain, speaking at a Conservative Party meeting in London on 4 April said that by not taking full advantage of German superiority in September, Hitler had 'missed the bus'.

Five days later, the Führer launched a double operation which he described as 'the boldest and most impudent in the history of warfare': Operation Weserübung Nord (Weser Crossing North), and Operation Weserübung Sud (Weser Crossing South), the simultaneous invasions of Norway and Denmark. While Britain promised military assistance to Norway, the Germans promised 'protection' to both Norway and Denmark.

The British Government's determination to back its promise to Norway angered Gort and his staff. Feeling that the Western Front was secure, the Prime Minister and War Office concentrated on Scandinavia and 15 Brigade was detached from the 5th Division for deployment in Norway. Ammunition supplies to the BEF in France ceased for a time and the arrival of III Corps in France was delayed.

French and British troops were hastily dispatched to Norway, but after some initial successes on land and sea, the campaign, which had been poorly planned and executed, started to go wrong. On 8 June, following events in France, the Allies were forced to evacuate.

In the immediate aftermath of Germany's invasion of Norway and Denmark, Britain and France approached the Belgian Government seeking permission for their troops to cross the border, but were once again refused. General Gamelin had a low opinion of the Belgians, an opinion he had made clear the previous October when he called them 'unthinking, short sighted mediocrities . . . in a large part to blame for Poland's obliteration; they have considerably handicapped Franco-British action when they could have helped in numerous ways . . . Belgium must bear a heavy responsibility – and she will pay for it by serving as the powers' battlefield.'

Harsh words but in reality both he and the Belgians were striving to achieve the same end. Neither country wanted another war to be fought on their soil after the suffering and destruction endured between 1914 and 1918. However, on 23 April, the Allies decided that even if Holland alone was the target of Hitler's next attack, the armies of Britain and France would cross the border irrespective of the Belgian Government's attitude.

For the Holy Boys, life went on much as before, although leave was suspended and the Battalion placed on six hours' notice to advance into Belgium.

'We didn't know much about Norway at all,' admitted Ernie Farrow. 'We had our own little goings on where we were and hardly knew what was going on anywhere else in the world; only around Orchies.'

Some of the men had a brief interlude from the usual routine when they swapped training and shovels for 'bull'. On Monday, 22 April, the Battalion was ordered to find a guard of honour for General Georges who was making a tour of the front line. 'A' Company was detailed to find clean clothing, khaki blanco and caps; the guard was to consist of Captain Barclay MC, Second Lieutenant Murray Brown and fifty other ranks. They were to be formed up at Marchiennes railway station at 1630 on the afternoon of the Wednesday the 24th. General Georges was suitably impressed. As he walked down the line, he remarked: 'That is what I call a guard.'

April also saw a change in corps commanders for the Norfolks. Sir John Dill returned to the UK to take up the position of Vice Chief of the Imperial General Staff; his replacement as commander of I Corps was Lieutenant General Michael 'Bubbles' Barker, who sadly was to lose his nerve in the later stages of the campaign.

For the men of the British Expeditionary Force, the 'Phoney War' was almost over. In Germany, three army groups were poised to launch *Fall Gelb*. Facing Holland and northern Belgium was General Fedor von Bock's Army Group B, consisting of twenty-nine divisions of which three were Panzer. In the centre, facing the Ardennes and Luxembourg, were the forty-five divisions, including seven Panzer, of Army Group A, commanded by General Gerd von Rundstedt. Opposite the Maginot Line was General Ritter von Leeb's Army Group C, whose seventeen divisions were to keep the French Army pinned down in that sector.

By this time both sides had reached near parity in manpower and arms. Including forty-five reserve divisions, the Germans had a total of 136 divisions; the French had 100 while the British contribution had risen to ten. If the Belgians' twenty-two and Dutch ten are taken into account, the Allied total was 142 divisions: some 3.7 million men as opposed to the Germany's 2.7 million.

As for the machinery of war, the Allies were superior in tank numbers. Against a German total of some 3,465 tanks, the French alone could field 3,680; the British had 300 and the Belgians 270.[5] What ultimately made the difference was the way in which they were used. The Allies spread their tanks thinly in what has been described as 'penny packets', largely as infantry support. The Germans, on the other hand, concentrated theirs into armoured spearheads which, closely supported by the Luftwaffe, would smash their way through opposing lines.

In the area of field artillery, the French possessed approximately 10,700 pieces against the *Wehrmacht*'s 7,400.

It was in the air that the Germans had superiority by a ratio of about two to one. The Luftwaffe's total of fighters, bombers and reconnaissance aircraft was 3,530. The French Air Force (Armée de l'Aire) was equipped with 1,286 aircraft. Between them the Dutch and Belgians could contribute 125 and 180 respectively, while the British had approximately 416 fighters and bombers operating in France with the BEF's Air Component and the Advanced Air Striking Force. Not only did the Germans enjoy the edge in numbers but as John Keegan has pointed out: 'The Luftwaffe was superior in quality of aircraft and in tactics of ground-air operations . . . and far superior in fighting experience to the Armée de l'Aire and the Advanced Air Striking Force of the RAF combined.'[6]

During the evening of Thursday, 9 May, a special train arrived in Euskirchen just south-west of Bonn and about 25 miles from Germany's border with Belgium. On board was Adolf Hitler, not heading for Hamburg and a shipyard inspection as believed, but to his new western field HQ ready for the launch of *Fall Gelb*. A further 12 miles by car brought him to the *Felsennest*, or Rocky Eyrie, as the HQ was named – a series of concrete bunkers blasted and hewn into the side of a tree-covered promontory.

The code word 'Danzig' had been transmitted to German commanders at 0900 that morning. His army knew what was expected of it. Hitler's message to them was:

The hour has come for the decisive battle for the future of the German nation. For three hundred years the rulers of England and France have made it their aim to prevent any real consolidation of Europe and above all to keep Germany weak and helpless. With this your hour has come. The fight which begins today will decide the destiny of the German people for a thousand years. Now do your duty.

Notes
1. Danchev and Todman, *War Diaries*, diary entry for 14 January 1940.
2. *Ibid.*, diary entry for 15 January 1940.
3. Montgomery, *Memoirs*.
4. *Ibid.*
5. Pallaud, John-Paul, *Blitzkrieg in the West, Then and Now*, Battle of Britain Prints, 1991. Such figures are notoriously difficult to ascertain with any accuracy, but these have been commended by historians as well researched.
6. Keegan, John, *The Second World War*, Hutchinson, 1989. Reprinted by permission of The Random House Group Ltd.

CHAPTER 4

'Give 'em a bloody nose, old boy, and then pull out!'

A T AROUND 0300 ON FRIDAY, 10 May 1940, the Belgian and Dutch governments received a communiqué from the Nazi Government, justifying its intention to violate the neutrality of its two neighbours. By entering their territories, the Germans were going to 'forestall a projected Anglo-French invasion'. An hour later, the British Ambassador in Brussels, Sir Lancelot Oliphant, was visited by Paul-Henri Spaak, the Belgian Foreign Minister, who appealed for British assistance.

Reports that an invasion was imminent had been reaching Brussels and Luxembourg from about 0100 onwards and were passed to the French at 0300. Army Intelligence was initially sceptical; there had been false alarms before and they wanted to be sure that the information was valid.

The Holy Boys appear to have been in a state of readiness during the night. Captain Charles Long, then of 'C' Company, in 'A War Diary' compiled while a prisoner of war wrote: 'Coy Commanders Conference 0300 – Coys to move to hide up Marchiennes Forest.'[1]

The Battalion's strength as given in the return of 5 May was 744 other ranks. The officers were listed by Captain Long as follows:

Bn HQ

Lieutenant Colonel de Wilton	CO
Major Charlton	2i/c
Major Marshall	Adjutant
Second Lieutenant Merritt	IO
Lieutenant Draffin	MO

HQ Coy

Major Ryder	OC
Captain Gordon	Signals Officer
A/Captain Hallett	MTO
Lieutenant Grant	QM
Second Lieutenant Elson	Carrier Platoon Commander
Second Lieutenant Buckingham	A/MTO

'A' Coy
Captain Barclay
Second Lieutenant Slater
Second Lieutenant Fulton

'B' Coy
Captain Allen
Lieutenant Yallop
Second Lieutenant Potter

'C' Coy
Captain Long
Lieutenant Woodwark
Lieutenant Edgeworth
Second Lieutenant Simpson
Second Lieutenant Willeson

'D' Coy
Major Richardson
Second Lieutenant Buchanan
Second Lieutenant Jones
Attached
Captain Hastings (Ox & Bucks Light Infantry)

Bde L O
Second Lieutenant Swainson

Other Officers of the Battalion

'A' Coy – Captain Gibbons	Leave
'A' Coy – Second Lieutenant Murray Brown	Course (UK)
'C' Coy – Captain Elwes	Leave
Padre – Captain Billups-Lea	MDS

At H-Hour, 0535 hrs, the *Wehrmacht* crossed the borders of neighbouring countries on a front stretching from north to south of some 300 miles. Paratroopers dropped into Holland and half an hour later glider-borne troops started their descent onto the Belgian fortress of Eben Emael (it fell the following day). The Luftwaffe flew deep into Allied territory attacking railways, airfields, headquarters buildings and supply points to disrupt and destroy.

French HQ ordered an alert at 0545, followed, around half an hour later, by a message from General Georges' HQ, that the order to execute Plan D had been given by the Supreme Commander.

BEF HQ accordingly sent out the following: 'Plan D.J.1. Today. Zero hour 1300 hours. 12L. may cross before zero. Wireless silence cancelled after crossing frontier. Command Post opens 1300 hours. Air recces may commence forthwith.'

In lay terms this translates to: 'Plan D comes into operation at 1300. 12th Lancers may cross the Franco-Belgian frontier before then. Wireless silence is cancelled after entering Belgium. The Commander-in-Chief's Command Post will open at Wahagnies [south of Lille, between Carvin and Orchies] at 1300. Air reconnaissance may commence forthwith.'[2]

At Orchies, the Norfolks made final preparations for the move. Their concentration area was to be near Beuvry-la-Forêt, some 2½ miles to the east, where they would find concealment in the Forêt de Sec Marais Marchiennes. Surplus baggage was taken to the brigade dump at Lecelles and the first men set out at 1030. The move was complete by early afternoon.

During the early afternoon and again in the evening, the town was attacked by the Luftwaffe. According to Second Lieutenant Jones 'at about 2.00 pm three German bombers arrived and planted their cargo of bombs on the station and level crossing at Orchies.' These targets were close to Divisional HQ.

For Captain Nick Hallett, the Motor Transport Officer, it was his 'first experience of this sort of thing, and decidedly unpleasant, as about 200 yards is much too close for comfort'.[3]

The attack served as a stark reminder that the 'Phoney War' was over; that on the other side of Belgium and in Holland men were fighting and dying in a forlorn bid to protect their home-lands from the full force of German aggression. For the moment the Holy Boys had escaped the Luftwaffe: 'They tried to bomb us but fortunately we're here,' Captain Barclay told his men while they waited in the forest, 'we beat them.'

In a few hours they would be setting off for the River Dyle; the 12th Lancers, in their light armoured cars, were already on their way, heading for positions 8 miles beyond the Dyle to observe approaches from the east. They were followed by the 4th/7th Royal Dragoon Guards, 13th/18th Royal Hussars, 15th/19th King's Royal Hussars and the 5th Royal Inniskilling Dragoon Guards. These mechanized units fulfilled what the commanders still referred to as the 'cavalry screen', operating in front of the main force.

At 1700, the Norfolks' Company Commanders were called together and details for the move into Belgium were given. The 4 Brigade Advance Guard and 2nd Division 'R' Group moved off at 1830.

Darkness had enveloped the forest when Barclay gathered the men of 'A' Company around him. By the light of a single hurri-cane lamp, he gave them, in the words of Ernie Leggett:

> a fatherly talk. The last words he said were, 'Now more than ever before, will your training stand you in good stead, keep your heads down and spirits high, and from now on when you aim your rifle to shoot, you shoot to kill!' They were ominous words. He then said, 'The best of luck, men!' After that we just formed up and marched away.

It was just after midnight when they left the cover of the forest and marched on to the main road which led to Valenciennes. Around 4 miles away their transport was waiting. Ahead lay a journey to the Dyle of 67 miles. They embussed at the Rosult crossroads, the engines roared into life and the convey set off steadily along the French roads. They passed through Rumegies, a place that had become so familiar to them, where the leading lorries crossed the frontier at Pont Cailloux at 0200 hrs.

'I felt very excited,' wrote Captain Hallett, 'as this was what we had been waiting for since the beginning of the war. Action was imminent.'[4]

Without the reassuring beam of headlights to guide them over unfamiliar Belgian roads, the way ahead could have been concealed by a close wall of darkness. They had trained and trained hard for night convoy driving but Murray Brown, although not with the Battalion at this time, explained in an article written after the war, how the problem was overcome: 'Divisional traffic control worked admirably, using small electric torches on the road side which proved invaluable as guiding lights. Despite driving with no lights until daylight, progress was steady and continuous.'

At around 0400, however, Captain Long said that there was a severe hold up which caused a delay of one and a half hours. Daylight brought with it the deadly threat of air attack.

Lord Gort was taking a calculated risk. Time was of such importance that he accepted that British 'air support might be insufficient to prevent interference with the move. Events were to prove the risk was justifiable.'

Orders regarding attack from the air were, according to Captain Hastings, quite definite: the troops were not to debus, the trucks were to press on regardless.[5] The Holy Boys braced themselves for what they had been warned was inevitable, but as Second Lieutenant Jones later wrote: 'the inevitable for some unaccountable reason did not happen.' Or did it? Ernie Farrow recalled that some of his fellow Norfolks said that lorries were machine-gunned on their way to the Dyle.

Bob Brown spoke of the move:

going quite well until part of the way through the morning [when] a German observation plane came over, a Storch, I believe they were called . . . he disappeared and not long after [that a] flight of bombers came over – I couldn't say at the time whether they were Heinkels or Dorniers. [They were not dive-bombers.] We immediately stopped the convoy and debussed into the sides of the roads. And they came and bombed the convoy but none of the vehicles were hit. They just dropped in the fields round the sides of them, so we were lucky for our first taste of warfare.

Brown thought that they were about halfway through Belgium at the time.

Captain Barclay also mentioned that they 'were attacked from the air once or twice with very little effect'.

Perhaps these attacks were simply token gestures, not designed to inflict heavy damage on the convoys because the Germans were working to a plan. They wanted the Allies to reach their positions on the Dyle.

'As in Poland,' Major General von Mellenthin explained, 'we enjoyed the advantage of air superiority, but no attempt was made to interfere with the British and French columns streaming into Belgium and southern Holland. The German High Command was delighted to see the enemy responding to our offensive in the exact manner which we desired and predicted.'[6]

'I could have wept for joy,' Hitler later revealed. 'They had fallen into the trap.'

That a trap had been sprung was foreseen by Lieutenant Colonel Paul de Villelume, military adviser to the French Premier. He told General Gamelin so and implored him to consider stopping the advance. Gamelin was unmoved, saying that when the decision was taken to go into Belgium they were prepared to accept all risks.

It was too late to help the Belgians by simply falling back onto the Escaut Plan.

The convoy of Norfolks headed steadily in a north-easterly direction, via Leuze-en-Hainut, Ath (Aat), Enghien (Edingen), Halle (Hal) and La Hulpe. 'Good traffic control,' observed Captain Long, 'good road discipline – route well policed and marked.'

The War Diary of 4th Infantry Brigade records that the 'Belgian people

throughout the advance showed all outward signs of enthusiasm and appeared to welcome the British troops.' Indeed this is rather understated as the welcome was very warm. Young children ran beside the trucks, flowers were thrown at the troops, and Belgian chocolates and cigarettes handed out. Whenever the convoy stopped, women came from their homes with hot cups of coffee for the Tommies.

While they were debussing near Tombeek and preparing to

make their way to their positions, a Heinkel flew over the stationary convoy. 'Some mad fool started firing a Bren gun at it,' wrote Second Lieutenant Jones. 'Within a few minutes every gun in the convoy was firing at it regardless of the fact it was miles out of range.'

The aircraft's height was estimated at 7,000 feet and when some pieces appeared to fall off several men were convinced that they had scored a hit. 'Of course they hadn't hit it at all,' Private Herbert Lines of the Carrier Platoon recalled, 'they were four bombs they were dropping! They splattered all around us.'

No damage was inflicted but the German pilot evidently reported back and the Norfolks suffered a subsequent raid. This time it was more determined, giving the Holy Boys their first experience of an aircraft designed not only to kill but to strike terror into those on the ground. Stuka dive-bombers, all fitted with screaming wind sirens, dropped out of the sky, stooping like birds of prey, bombing and strafing. Some found the sirens much worse than the noise of machine-guns and bombs, and placed their fingers in their ears in the hope of blocking out that banshee howl. William O'Callaghan said that he tried to screw himself up to the size of a matchbox when the bombers came.[7]

As the advance guard, the Holy Boys were initially on their own in the brigade sector. 'Position overlooking swamps of R. Dyle,' wrote Captain Long. 'Bn dug in or occupied existing trenches and blockhouses – Keys of most concrete posts missing.'

'D' Company dug in at the foot of tree-covered slopes which fell quite steeply to the banks of the Dyle. The Company Commander, Major Richardson, and Captain Hastings, who was on second-ment from the Oxfordshire and Buckinghamshire Light Infantry, remained at the top of the slope overlooking the men's positions and spent the night in the open.[8]

Second Lieutenant Jones considered their position to be a good one. He felt that the river formed 'a good Anti-Tank obstacle, it was well wired and there were several very good Belgian Pill Boxes and semi-dug trenches'.

In the course of the night, the two other battalions of 4th Infantry Brigade reached the sector and formed a three-battalion front, north of and including Wavre. The 1st Royal Scots were on the right, the 1st/8th Lancashire Fusiliers in the centre with the

Norfolks on the left. The Brigade's War Diary stated that they were 'covering the whole of the Divisional front'.

Wavre was at the southern end of the British sector, the right flank, and marked the junction between the BEF and French First Army. (A map illustrating the positions as they were on 15 May shows the boundary between the British and French forces as running right through Wavre.)

When the 4th Infantry Brigade took up their positions during the night of 11/12 May, General Blanchard's First Army had not yet arrived. The Gembloux Gap was covered by a 'cavalry screen' of two French light mechanized divisions: DLMs or Division Légèrie Mécanique, equipped with tanks, and commanded by General Prioux. Prioux was shocked when he arrived to see just how poor the Belgian defences were. He immediately sent messages to both General Billotte and General Georges asking for Plan D to be abandoned and Plan E implemented, but his request was turned down. The French Seventh Army, on the extreme left of the Allied line, and the BEF were well on their way to their objectives. It was decided that the speed of Blanchard's advance should be increased by twenty-four hours bringing his force into position on 14 May.

'A' Company under the irrepressible Peter Barclay was to take up the outpost position on the eastern or enemy side of the River Dyle, while the rest of the Battalion remained on the western side. His orders were, in his own succinct words: 'Give 'em a bloody nose, old boy, and then pull out.'

His task was to cover the main road leading to a bridge which crossed the Dyle. His front was about 600 yards looking out across open, quite undulating, countryside which gave him a good view of anything approaching. The area he chose to site his positions offered 'a lot of cover' amongst the shrubbery in the gardens of a small chateau, where, of all things, a garden party was in progress. Children were dancing around a maypole providing a scene of peaceful, carefree normality – while further east the German Army was smashing its way across the Albert Canal. The lady of the house was horrified when Barclay informed her of his intention to dig trenches in and around her garden.

'As long as you don't upset the rose bushes,' she said, 'and as long as you don't interfere with the rhododendrons too much, I suppose I can't stop you.'

'Well,' said Barclay, 'I should certainly curtail your garden party activities and send all these kids home because there's going to be all hell let loose here in the next day or two. And I suggest the children are better at home.'

'Not to worry,' she countered, 'my husband will let me know if there is any need for alarm.'

'Where is he?' Barclay asked.

'He's in Brussels,' came the reply.

'Well, you can't get through to Brussels now,' Barclay informed her, 'because all the lines are down; fifth columnists have been at work or something, but all the lines are down. There's no chance of getting him on the phone.'

While the garden party continued, 'A' Company dug in. Barclay later recalled:

I had slit trench positions based on the platoon, three sections in each platoon. And I had, in fact, two platoons up and one platoon back. They had a very good field of fire from the positions of this chateau's garden. We covered this road from jolly good concealed positions which we were able to prepare quite quickly and camouflage over, a vital finale to any digging, any trench digging operation.

During the morning of Sunday, 12 May, the Norfolks' main positions west of the Dyle were reconnoitered by 1st Battalion Royal Berkshire Regiment from 6 Brigade. At 2100 hrs the previous evening, Brigadier Warren had called a conference and according to the 4th Infantry Brigade War Diary: 'Operation Order No. 2 was issued. The operation order covered the handing over of the left half of the Divisional front to 6th Infantry Brigade and the sidestepping of 2/Norfolks to Brigade reserve.'

At midday, the Holy Boys commenced the move to their new positions above Wavre in the rear of the Bois de Beaumont. Already they could hear heavy gunfire to the north-east – gunfire which grew steadily louder as the hours ticked by, measuring in sound the inexorable German advance. The Belgian fortress of Eben Emael had fallen the previous day; vital bridges had been taken and held despite valiant Belgian attempts to dislodge them; German paratroopers had virtually cut Holland in two, and much of the Dutch Army was falling back towards Rotterdam and Amsterdam away from the projected Allied line. Although advance elements of General Giraud's Seventh Army had reached Breda on 11 May, the planned link-up with the Dutch forces was now impossible. On the BEF's right, the 3rd and 4th Panzer Divisions of General Höppner's XVI Panzer Corps were striking out for the Gembloux Gap.

Before the advancing German tide came displaced civilians, their towns, villages and homes engulfed, desperately seeking sanctuary behind the Allies – hoping, praying that the armies of France, Britain and their own country would hold the line, a line that meant the difference between freedom and oppression, life and death. Among them were Belgian soldiers, battered remnants of units that had tried to defend their frontiers but had been over-whelmed. Numbers gradually increased. From their outpost in the chateau gardens, Barclay's men watched the melancholy retreat. Gunfire grew louder, the distance ever shorter . . . how much time? Hours, perhaps minutes only, before the field-grey uniforms appeared.

West of the Dyle, the Norfolks found that progress to their new positions was hampered by civilians. 'Movement along the roads,' recorded the Regimental History, 'was made very difficult by the evacuation of civilians, and it was noticed that among them were a large number of Belgian soldiers moving to the rear, apparently disorganized. Their appearance, coupled with the sound of heavy artillery fire, caused a good deal of apprehension.'

Captain Hastings recalled that he saw thousands of Belgian troops. 'All the soldiers looked unkempt, and were unshaven, and the eyes of many were shining and staring as if they had been through a frightening experience.' One Belgian officer told Lieutenant Yallop that his Company Commander had been killed and the Second in Command turned and ran followed by the rest of the company.[9]

During the afternoon, there was a gas scare but Brigade HQ could obtain no information. 'It was reported later,' concluded the War Diary, 'that the scare was caused by an ammonia factory catching fire.'

After a quiet night, work resumed on digging and wiring the new positions. Wavre was attacked by the Luftwaffe during the morning and several houses were set on fire, but the Norfolks suffered no casualties. Luckily they also took no casualties when a few shells fired from long range dropped close to their positions. In the evening, British artillery opened fire, ranging on a hillside east of the Dyle. When official confirmation came through that the Germans were across the Albert Canal in strength, it is probably true to say that it came as no real surprise. Ever increasing numbers of Belgian soldiers and their vehicles, and the fleeing civilians, provided testimony enough.

The men of 'A' Company probably made their way back to the Battalion's positions west of the river during the night of 13/14 May as the Brigade War Diary states that all outposts were withdrawn that night.

As ordered, the Germans had been given 'a bloody nose' by Barclay's company. The enemy vanguard had consisted of motorcycle combinations, the sidecars fitted with machine-guns, obviously the 'forward eyes' of the main formation.

Barclay had allowed them to get 'jolly close because we wanted to get as many as we could. I think the leading one was only about a hundred and fifty yards away.' The Germans were taken completely by surprise. 'We knocked out about four or five . . . in fact, none of the first batch that appeared got back to report.' But Barclay could see in the distance the build-up of enemy forces:

> It obviously didn't take long before the follow-up troops smelt a rat and we were subjected to a great deal of fire, heavy mortar and artillery fire . . . In fact, the positions on the west bank of the river came under a good deal more fire than our positions on the enemy side of the river . . . And then, how long, I can't remember, but I think after first contact was established, we were there for about four or five hours. Then darkness fell and we were ordered to pull out under the cover of darkness and cover the bridge-blowing party [Royal Engineers] after we'd crossed over . . . Then we came home and moved into Reserve position to the battalion on the battalion sector.

With Höppner's panzers driving for the Gembloux Gap, and the French First Army still on its way, the BEF's right flank could have been fatally exposed. Near the village of Hannut, some 16 miles north-east of Gembloux, the Germans ran into the 'cavalry screen' provided by the DLMs of General Prioux. Between 12 and 14 May, French tanks fought German Panzers. Initially, the French scored a victory, stopping the Germans in their tracks. One hundred and sixty-five Panzers were knocked out to the French 105, but their success was short-lived. When Blanchard's First Army reached its objective during the afternoon of 14 May, Prioux withdrew his DLMs and fell back behind the lines. This left the field to the Germans who were able to recover and repair around a hundred of their Panzers while the damaged French tanks were lost.

Allied air reconnaissance revealed that the German forces were moving rapidly – speed was of the essence to von Reichneau's Sixth Army. His instructions, according to the War Diary of Army Group B, stressed the importance of breaking 'through the enemy positions between Louvain and Namur in order to prevent French and Belgian forces establishing themselves in this position'.

The 'cavalry screen' of the BEF withdrew across the Dyle during the morning of 14 May, 4th/7th Royal Dragoon Guards passing through the Norfolks' lines. Enemy units were soon seen on the far bank of the river, checking abandoned British positions. Bridges were blown, one with a party of Germans about halfway across. As Allied artillery, guided by spotter aircraft, fired on the eastern bank, German dive-bombers attacked units of the French First Army as they moved into position on the right. The Royal Scots were already in contact with enemy infantry at Wavre but the Holy Boys only suffered light shellfire. According to Captain Long, there was 'no enemy activity during the night but Allied gunfire was incessant'.

On the morning of 15 May, when the Dutch Army formally capitulated, the *Wehrmacht* attempted to press home its attack along the whole BEF front. The German IV Corps, supported by the Luftwaffe, attacked the 2nd Division's sector near Wavre which, itself occupied by the Royal Scots, had been severely bombed the previous day. The Holy Boys had completed the digging and tactical wiring of their defensive positions and were ready. When the Stukas attacked, 'C' Company claimed a kill by bringing one down with Bren-gun fire.

Ernie Farrow, who was part of the 28-strong Pioneer Platoon at HQ Company, recalled a German sniper pinning his platoon down for about an hour. The men hardly dared to move. Concealed in a building some 200 yards away, the threat was eventually removed when the Mortar Platoon plastered the sniper's position.[10]

German shells were now dropping in 'D', 'C' and HQ Company areas, and in the vicinity of Battalion HQ. 'C' Company suffered three casualties: two wounded and one killed.

The heaviest attacks appeared to be going in against the French forces on the right where the First Moroccan and 1st Motorized divisions were now in position in the Gembloux Gap. The Moroccan Division, Julian Jackson wrote: 'was only a partially motorized unit that had covered 135 km of the journey on foot. The last soldiers only arrived on the morning of 14 May and were still preparing their positions, under enemy air attack, when the German tanks moved against them'[11]

The French were being hard pressed and during the afternoon of 15 May, their junction with the BEF was supposedly breeched. A report reached the Norfolks that a French colonial unit had been broken and had retreated in some disorder. The flank of the 4th Infantry Brigade and indeed the whole BEF was in danger of being exposed near the village of Bierges, which lies just north-west of Wavre. Bierges itself was reported to be in enemy hands. 'A' and 'C' companies were moved up to deal with the situation; 'A' was to attack while 'C' was to cover the rear of the village and support 'A' Company if necessary.

According to Captain Barclay's version of events, when he was sent for by his Commanding Officer, Lieutenant Colonel de Wilton 'seemed to be in rather a state'. He told Barclay that the Germans had crossed the river on the right.

'They'll have come under fairly heavy fire if that happened,' Barclay pointed out.

'Oh, yes, they have,' said de Wilton.

Barclay found this very strange because the Adjutant, Major Marshall, appeared to know nothing about it, but de Wilton reckoned that he had received a message from a dispatch rider from Brigade.

'I want you to recapture that village over there,' continued de Wilton.

'That's a French Reserve Division,' Barclay countered. 'I mean, if they're over in that village, they must be in visual range of any enemy over there.'

'Oh,' said the Commanding Officer, 'they're all right; you've got to go and recapture it.'

It took Barclay about an hour to plan his attack. Initial reconnaissance was not too difficult as the ground between the Norfolks' position and their objective could be seen. Platoon commanders were then briefed.

'We prepared a fire plan,' Barclay explained, 'with artillery fire coming down on this place hot and strong; machine-guns [2nd Battalion The Manchester Regiment, a machine-gun battalion] from very good positions slightly to the flank; mortars the lot.' Barclay then discussed his plan 'with the Adjutant rather than the Commanding Officer because the Adjutant made more sense'.

The artillery bombardment lasted for around ten minutes and 'A' Company's platoons leapfrogged forward: 'I had two platoons forward and one back and I had each platoon advancing with the other platoon giving close fire support.'

It did not taken them long to cover the thousand yards from the start line. When they were about a 150 yards from the village, they prepared for the final assault – a bayonet charge.

'There'd been no retaliatory fire coming at all,' Barclay said, 'which seemed very surprising to me because I thought, you know, that the fire plan had obviously been so sound and so effective that it had kept all the heads down. And just as we were going to put in the final assault, to my astonishment, a British carrier emerged from the village.'

At first he thought that the Germans had captured it and were about to use it against the attackers. He ordered the soldier who was equipped with the company's Boyes anti-tank rifle to conceal himself behind a nearby bank, keep the safety catch on, train it on the carrier but not to fire until ordered. As the carrier drew nearer, Barclay saw a man wearing a British tin hat stand up and wave a walking stick. It was Lieutenant Colonel Money, Commanding Officer of the Royal Scots.

'What the devil do you think you're up to?' he yelled.

'We are just recapturing this village,' returned Barclay.

'What the devil do you want to do that for? I was in the middle of having the best meal I've had since war broke out with the Brigadier in charge of the French Brigade in that sector, and suddenly shells started pouring through the roof and brought the delectable meal to a summary halt.'

By this time daylight was fading, so Money told Barclay to stay in the village with the Scots until he got things sorted out with his battalion and he could go back and rejoin them in the morning.

Lieutenant Colonel de Wilton had totally misjudged the situation. Barclay's assessment was that his Commanding Officer was actually 'in a very high state of excitement and wrought nervousness [and] had imagined this thing had happened'. Such was his mental state that he 'was convinced the village had been captured and it was Reserve company's job to retake it.'

In summarizing the day, the Regimental History had this to say:

> All seemed to be going well. Casualties were very light and nowhere had the enemy been able to break through. The dangerous situation on the right flank had been restored by the recapture of Bierges, and it came therefore as a surprise when orders were received in the evening to retire to a new line on the River Lasne, in the neighbourhood of Overyssche [Overijse].

A breech of some 5,000 yards had been made on the French First Army's front according to the British Official History. In order to restore the situation, Lord Gort offered to send a brigade from the 48th (South Midland) Division which was being held in I Corps reserve. General Billotte declined; instead he issued orders to General Blanchard to pull his First Army back and form a new line running from Ottignies southwards to Châtelet, which lies just east of Charleroi. Billotte may well have been reacting to an unexpected situation which had occurred further south on the River Meuse.

British I Corps now had to adjust its line to conform to Blanchard's forces. Thus, pivoting roughly on St-Agatha-Rode on the Dyle, the right had to swing back to create a new line running north-east to south-west, along the River Lasne. Good defensive positions were abandoned as the Wavre sector of the Dyle front was evacuated. Roads were mined and at approximately midnight the Holy Boys moved out with 'D' Company, less 17 Platoon under Platoon Sergeant Major Hodson, which had been sent out to investigate rumours of a German parachute landing, covering the Battalion. At 0700 on Thursday, 16 May, they were in position between La Hulpe and Overijse.

The Brigade was now deployed on a three-battalion front: Lancashire Fusiliers on the left, Norfolks in the centre and Royal Scots on the right. Battalion HQ was established in a chateau near Maliezen: 'B', 'C' and 'D' were the forward companies with 'A' in reserve.

'The first report received on 16th,' says the Regimental History, 'was that a bridge across the river at Tombeek had been left standing. B Company was hurriedly loaded into MT and set out for the village, finding the bridge and destroying it.'

Much of the day was spent in resting and again preparing positions. There was no contact with the enemy but a British Lysander aircraft was shot down by two German aircraft near 'C' Company's position.

In the early afternoon, four very wet and bedraggled men from 'A' Company reached the battalion lines having swum across the River Lasne – during the withdrawal the previous night, the quartet had been left behind in Wavre. While loading a lorry, they were surprised by the sudden appearance of a German cavalry unit, but in the confusion of the brief firefight that followed, they managed to escape and find their way to the new positions.

These positions, however, would only be held for a few more hours. Towards evening, new orders were received for a further withdrawal. Some 75 miles to the south, 'a sinister bulge', as Winston Churchill put it, had appeared in the French front at Sedan. Gerd von Rundstedt's Army Group A had broken through on the River Meuse.

Notes

1. Long, Captain Charles, '2nd Royal Norfolk Regiment, A War Diary 10–28 May 1940', compiled while a POW, December 1941; reproduced by kind permission of the Trustees of the Royal Norfolk Regimental Museum, Norwich. Long/War Diary.
2. Ellis, *The War in France and Flanders*.

3. Sebag-Montefiore, Hugh, *Dunkirk: Fight to the Last Man*, Viking, 2006. Quotes from Captain Nick Hallett's memoir: 'A Diary of the Blitzkrieg and After: May 1940'. Reproduced with permission of Curtis Brown Ltd., London, on behalf of Hugh Sebag-Montefiore; copyright Hugh Sebag-Montefiore.
4. *Ibid.*
5. Sebag-Montefiore, *Dunkirk*. Quotes from Captain R.J. Hastings' memoir: 'Recollections of the Blitz'.
6. Mellenthin, *Panzer Battles*.
7. Jolly, *The Vengeance of Private Pooley*.
8. Sebag-Montefiore, *Dunkirk*.
9. *Ibid.*
10. Jolly, *The Man who Missed the Massacre*.
11. Jackson, Julian, *The Fall of France: The Nazi Invasion of 1940*, OUP, 2003; from page 161 by permission of Oxford University Press.

CHAPTER 5

'Why can't we fight it out?'

I N THE EARLY HOURS OF 15 MAY 1940, Winston Churchill, who
had succeeded Chamberlain as Prime Minister five days before,
was awakened by a telephone call from the French Premier, Paul
Reynaud. The news was grim. Reynaud told Churchill that they
had been defeated, that the front at Sedan had been breeched and
that German armour and mechanized units were pouring through
in strength.[1]

At 1730 the following afternoon, the British Prime Minister
arrived at the Quai d'Orsay, the French Foreign Ministry, for a
meeting with French leaders. In the gardens, bonfires were burning
and wheelbarrow loads of state documents were being added to the
flames; a nation believing itself to be facing defeat was destroying
archives so they would not fall into enemy hands.

Churchill was shown a map illustrating the Allied front. At Sedan
there was 'a small but sinister bulge'. When Churchill asked
General Gamelin the whereabouts of the reserves, the reply was
that there were none. After a long pause, Churchill then asked
where and when he proposed to attack the flanks of the German
breakthrough. But Gamelin appeared to be at a loss about what to
do next, claiming that he did not have the manpower and that both
his equipment and methods were inferior.[2] In essence, he was
defeated.

While the Allies were busy reinforcing the front door, the
Germans had squeezed in through the side entrance, having crossed
terrain considered very difficult for a mechanized attack – the
Ardennes. Moving armoured and motorized divisions through this
thickly forested region of hills and valleys, served by only a few
minor, twisting roads, created long winding columns several miles

71

in length, vulnerable for their restriction of manoeuvre. It was risky but central to the revised German plan of attack.

When Hitler had ordered the immediate revision of *Fall Gelb* following Major Reinberger's disastrous flight, the strategy came not from the German High Command but a brilliant 52-year-old Lieutenant General, Chief of Staff, Army Group A. He had already outlined his plan in no less than six memoranda to Franz Halder. His persistence had so tried Halder's patience that the officer in question was promoted to command a corps in East Prussia, effectively getting him out of the way.

It was the custom, however, for newly appointed corps commanders to meet the Head of State as a ceremonial mark of respect. Rudloph Schmundt, Hitler's *Wehrmacht* Adjutant, was given details of the plan. Realizing how close it came to the Führer's own thinking (Hitler had suggested an attack through the Ardennes in October), Schmundt arranged for Erich von Manstein to have a longer meeting with Hitler on 17 February than protocol usually allowed.

In Manstein's plan, Army Group B would still launch an offensive against Belgium and Holland, but with a reduced force of twenty-nine divisions instead of forty-three. Their task was to draw what the Germans expected to be the cream of the Allied Army – the BEF and France's best armoured and mobile divisions – towards them. Major General von Mellenthin wrote:

> The advance of Army Group B would be formidable, noisy and spectacular; it would be accompanied by the dropping of parachute troops at key points in Belgium and Holland. There was little doubt that the enemy would regard this advance as the main attack and would move rapidly across the Franco-Belgian frontier in order to reach the line of the Meuse and cover Brussels and Antwerp. The more they committed themselves to this sector, the more certain would be their ruin.[3]

Basil Liddell Hart's much used analogy of 'the matador's cloak' well describes Army Group B's role.

Army Group A would now be responsible for executing the main attack through the Ardennes and across the River Meuse. Its spearheads would then head for the Channel coast thus cutting off the

Allied forces in Belgium. The size of Army Group A was increased from twenty-two divisions to forty-five.

The cutting edge of Group A's force were seven Panzer divisions which would have to make their way through the Ardennes. French war games carried out during the 1930s suggested that the 70 miles from the German border through the Ardennes to the Meuse would take a large armoured force about nine or ten days. German war games, on the other hand, arrived at an estimated time of sixty hours, which proved accurate, as Guderian's panzers took fifty-seven hours.

Lieutenant General Heinz Guderian, commander of XIX Panzer Corps, was the German Army's foremost proponent of armoured warfare. His concept formed the basis of what Western journalists had dubbed 'blitzkrieg'. Concentrating Panzers into large formations, where their firepower was at its most intense, provided the spearhead of the attack, battering their way through opposing defence lines. Because the Panzers were expected to continue their advance, motorized infantry followed in their wake to consolidate the breakthrough and mop up any remaining defenders. The Panzers themselves were supported by armoured engineering units, mobile artillery and anti-tank units to cover against counter-attacks. Much of the surprise element was provided by the Luftwaffe which replaced the field artillery's 'softening-up' role. A prolonged preliminary artillery barrage, as was the case in the First World War, gave away the attacker's intention.

In 1937, Guderian had published his ideas on tank warfare in *Achtung Panzer!* But as Peter Caddick-Adams has pointed out, 'at the time of its publication it was ignored by the British and French . . . Yet within its pages is a blueprint of Guderian's part in the invasion and defeat of France.'[4]

Ironically, Guderian acknowledged the influence of the British theories in the development of his concept:

It was principally the books and articles of the Englishmen, Fuller, Liddell Hart and Martel, that excited my interest and gave me food for thought. I learned from them the concentration of armour, as employed in the battle of Cambrai. Further, it was Liddell Hart who emphasized the use of armoured forces forlong-range strokes, operations against the opposing army's communications, and also proposed a type of armoured division combining panzer and panzer-infantry units.

Conservative elements within the British Army ensured that the new-fangled tank ideas never really got off the ground – until, that is, it was too late. Guderian, too, was faced with a similar attitude amongst German commanders.

'Tank armour prevents men from saluting properly on parade,' Fedor von Bock told him. 'Anyway you move too fast. How can you command all that without telephones?'

'By radio,' Guderian replied.

'Wrong!' retorted von Bock. 'Wireless will never work in a tank.'

It certainly did work. Guderian had been a signals specialist during the First World War and used his knowledge to the full, ensuring that all his Panzers, command vehicles and support units communicated by wireless. In his battle with the conservative elements he had one great advantage over his British counterparts: a Commander-in-Chief, Adolf Hitler, who enthusiastically embraced his ideas.

Facing the Germans along the River Meuse were the French Ninth and Second armies. They were certainly not first-rate units and in some areas were undermanned and poorly equipped. Criticism has often been levelled at their performance, and while some units buckled and retreated, others did their best. The German crossing of the Meuse, although quick, was not achieved with the ease that is sometimes implied.

By evening on 12 May, 7th Panzer Division, commanded by General Erwin Rommel, controlled the east bank of the Meuse near Dinant. During the evening infantry units managed to push across. But Rommel's forces subsequently met such fierce resistance that he feared some of his men were on the verge of losing their nerve.

Further south, at Monthermé, French defenders managed to hold up a Panzer Division for two days, while at Sedan Guderian described his crossing as 'almost a miracle'. Mostly the crossings were achieved by small units, led by extremely courageous individuals. Luck rode with the Germans.

Towards the end of 13 May, three somewhat tenuous bridge-heads had been established on the Meuse. Three days later they had consolidated into the 'sinister bulge' – a penetration into France, at its widest point, of some 59 miles.

It was little wonder that when Churchill met the French leaders they were in such a state of despondency. The speed of the break-through had thrown them into complete disarray; a grave miscalculation had been made. Although the Ardennes had never been wholly ruled out as an attack route, the crucial factor was time; the French had been convinced that 'there would be time to reinforce the sector before the Germans were ready to cross the river.'[5]

Without a full-strength, first-class reserve, much of which was in northern Belgium, the French were now forced to redeploy. The First Army would have to fall back. Gamelin had committed his best to the Dyle line believing Army Group B to pose the major threat. Yet in October 1939, according to the British Official History, he had told the CIGS, Sir Edmund Ironside, that he:

> expected a pinning down attack on the Maginot Line . . . He expected this to be accompanied by an attack across the western frontier of Luxembourg into the Ardennes, sweeping south of the Meuse . . . against the whole length of the Belgian frontier, south of the Meuse to Namur then across the Meuse and south of the Sambre to Charleroi. The German right would extend out perhaps to Valenciennes.

Sir Edmund added: 'General Gamelin spoke with great clarity.'

Like their Allied counterparts, the Germans were no less surprised by the initial success – they had gambled and won the first round. In March, Franz Halder had urged von Rundstedt to stick with the plan, believing that if the chance of success was as little as 10 per cent, it was the only way which would lead to the defeat of the enemy.

Senior German commanders, however, were growing increasingly nervous. Guderian was noted for his speed of advance; even his own men referred to him as 'Fast Heinz'. Concern mounted that his flanks would become exposed; as Churchill so graphically put it: 'The tortoise has protruded its head dangerously far from its shell' – at Guderian's speed, some tortoise.

On 17 May, General Ewald von Kleist, under whose command

Guderian's Panzer Corps came, ordered a halt. Peter Caddick-Adams wrote:

> Keen to exploit the success of his now nearly exhausted divisions, Guderian actually ignored this order and, when reprimanded by von Kleist, he submitted his resignation in disgust at not being allowed to continue the advance. Though initially accepted, this resignation was later refused, and indeed with von Kleist's connivance, Guderian was allowed to continue with a 'reconnaissance in force' during 17–18 May.[6]

Lord Gort wrote:

> By 16 May, it became clear that a prolonged defence of the Dyle position was impracticable. The French First Army on my right were unlikely to make good the ground lost on the previous day, notwithstanding the support I had given them in the air and on the ground, and a further withdrawal seemed likely to be forced on them by events in the south.

At 1000, Gort received orders from General Billotte's HQ for withdrawal to the River Escaut, taking up positions there as originally planned.

'The operation,' Gort explained, 'was to begin on the night of 16/17 May, one day being spent on the Senne [Brussels-Charleroi Canal] and one day on the Dendre positions; thus the Escaut would be reached on the night of 18/19 May, though French orders did not rule out the possibility of staying longer than one day on each bound.'

During the BEF's early days in France, Lieutenant Langley of the 2nd Battalion Coldstream Guards had asked his company commander why they repeatedly practised retreat and rearguard actions. The senior officer's response was to prove prophetic: 'We always start a war with a retreat. What makes you think it will be different this time?' After all, their predecessors in the BEF of 1914 had begun their war by retreating from Mons.

Towards evening on the 16th, the Holy Boys received orders to fall back from the River Lasne to the Brussels-Charleroi Canal.

Each battalion in the brigade supplied an officer and ten men, who remained behind to give the appearance that the British were still there in strength. While the major part of the brigade began their retirement through the Forêt de Soignes, the decoys moved up and down the main road by the river. It was an old ruse but appeared to work as the withdrawal was unhindered. What also probably helped was the Germans' initial failure to break through on the Dyle front. Army Group B was under instructions 'to follow up their thrust forthwith' if the Allies tried to escape, but von Bock had given orders for a 'prepared attack' to be mounted on 17 May.

Shortage of transport meant that available lorries soon became overloaded with equipment, some of which had to be discarded. Needless to say there was no room for the men and so they had to do what the 'poor bloody infantry' has always done, foot-slog their way towards their new positions. As dusk fell over the Forêt de Soignes, the Holy Boys joined a sad and jumbled procession of transport, soldiers and civilians moving west.

'Owing to lack of road and traffic control,' wrote Captain Long, 'considerable confusion during hours of darkness – maps out of date – route not marked.'

In an attempt to keep moving through such chaos some companies abandoned the main routes to try their luck on the side roads. In the darkness some became disorientated and inadvertently doubled back, only to find other companies heading in the opposite direction. After a 17-mile slog they came across the welcome sight of their transport. Having off-loaded the equipment in the new sector, the lorries had returned to lift the men.

Their positions at Loth by the Brussels-Charleroi Canal were reached at 0800 the following morning. There was little time for rest. After a hurried breakfast in an orchard near Loth, they set out for Ribstraat near Grammont (Geraardsbergen) on the River Dendre.

'There was no time to make out a brigade march table,' says the Regimental History, 'and units were ordered to make their way to Grammont as best they could.'

Before the Battalion moved off, the Luftwaffe attacked. 'D' Company was hit particularly badly; caught within the confines of a narrow defile, escape from the strafing and bombing was almost impossible and they suffered several casualties. Nearby, anti-aircraft units fought back, their Bofors guns bringing down two of the attackers.

The Luftwaffe, however, did not concentrate all their efforts on retreating soldiers – the masses of refugees clogging the roads were regarded as targets. In an arrogant display of armed aggression, Göring's pilots slaughtered helpless, unarmed men, women and children, not only to try and hinder the progress of the Allied troops, but also to undermine morale. Ernie Farrow vividly recalled three Stukas flying over the column. The men dived for cover but were completely ignored. Presently, he heard the cacophony of aerial attack in the distance: screaming sirens, the clatter of heavy calibre machine-guns and the blast of bombs. His first thought was that the attack had been directed against a unit of retreating Belgian soldiers:

> But, after we'd driven down the road three or four miles, we found what they'd done. They'd come over us, left us. But to stop us, they'd machine-gunned and bombed these poor refugees. This was a massacre. All along the road were people who had been killed, with no arms, no heads, there was cattle lying about dead, there was tiny little children; there was old people; not one or two people but hundreds of them lying about in the road. This was absolutely a massacre. We couldn't stop to clear the road, because we knew that this is what it was done for – to make us stop and the Germans would have surrounded us. So we had to drive our lorries over the top of them. Which was heartbreaking – really heart-breaking – for us but we couldn't do anything about it.

By 1900 hrs that evening, the River Dendre had been crossed and the Norfolks were fortunate enough to go straight into reserve. This gave them a chance to grab some much-needed sleep in the relative comfort of barns, outbuildings and even houses. In the seven days since the German invasion there had scarcely been time for rest. Some of the men found themselves falling asleep while marching. Ernie Leggett remembered doing so during a march of some 25 miles in darkness. 'People say you can't march while you're asleep. Well I can tell you here and now you can march while you're asleep because I've done it, and all my company ['A' Company] did it! The

Eric Hayes, who Peter Barclay described as 'a good skipper', commanded the 2nd Battalion until posted in January 1940. (*Courtesy Royal Norfolk Regimental Museum, Norwich*)

Peter Barclay commanded 'A' Company until wounded and evacuated in May 1940.
(*Courtesy Royal Norfolk Regimental Museum, Norwich*)

George Gristock, posthumously awarded the Victoria Cross (August 1940) for his gallantry during the fighting on the River Escaut during May 1940.
(*Courtesy Royal Norfolk Regimental Museum, Norwich*)

'That's what I call a guard', said General Georges as he inspected a Guard of Honour provided by the 2nd Norfolks at Marchiennes on 24 April 1940. *(Imperial War Museum, F 3977)*

Captain Peter Barclay re-enacts, for the press photographers, the moment his patrol set out for Waldwisse on the Saar Front in January 1940. (*Imperial War Museum, F 2274*)

The 2nd Battalion's last headquarters. (*Courtesy Royal Norfolk Regimental Museum, Norwich*)

The massacre site on Louis Creton's farm. (*Courtesy Royal Norfolk Regimental Museum, Norwich*)

Taken by a Frenchman shortly after the massacre, the photograph shows local people tending the mass grave of the 97 victims in the shadow of Louis Creton's barn. (*Courtesy Royal Norfolk Regimental Museum, Norwich*)

The mass grave, a melancholy yet fitting tribute created by the people of Le Paradis until the bodies were removed. (*Courtesy Royal Norfolk Regimental*

The victims of the massacre were exhumed in May 1942 and transferred to the communal cemetery in Le Paradis. (*Courtesy Royal Norfolk Regimental Museum, Norwich*)

The Creton Farm, 2004. (*Richard Lane*)

The Creton Farm and memorial which states in both English and French: 'At this spot 97 all ranks of the Royal Norfolk and other Regiments were massacred on 27th May 1940'. (*Richard Lane*)

only time you wake up is when you bump into the man ahead of you or the man behind you bumps into you.'

Concerns over Lieutenant Colonel de Wilton's health came to a head during the withdrawal – stress and the resulting lack of sleep had borne down heavily upon him. Impaired judgment had already led to the futile attack on Bierges and perhaps deep down de Wilton himself knew it. He had admitted to Captain Hastings that he felt very tired and was unsure of how much longer he could go on.[7]

It was Major Marshall who eventually managed to persuade de Wilton to be evacuated. 'He simply couldn't sleep,' said Barclay, 'and was so worn out that the doctor gave him a very good sleeping pill – sleeping dose – and without much opposition they managed to persuade him to go and have a bit more treatment.' Early on the morning of the 18th, de Wilton's leadership of the Holy Boys came to an end and he was evacuated.

As much as Barclay liked and admired him, he was critical of his appointment to command the Battalion:

> I know in the First World War which he saw a month or two of, he had to be evacuated from supposed shell-shock then. And it was a most awful pity that that lesson wasn't learned and he was used purely on the training side in the Second World War because he was a wonderful officer on the training side, and . . . a very charming gentleman. And that he should have cracked up like he did was a tragedy and could, I think, have been avoided . . .
>
> He was given various staff jobs but he was never the same man again. I mean, he knew that he'd let the side down and it really worked on his conscience forever and he died not so long after the war. And I can't help feeling that probably his demise was precipitated by his feelings of sadness.

Major Nicolas Charlton took over command with Major Lisle Ryder promoted to Second in Command. Captain Long was appointed OC HQ Company.

'And we carried on just as before,' said Barclay. 'In actual fact one of the records in the War Diary states the company commanders were such a good team and knew each other's form so well, they pretty well knew how to cope with any predictable situation;

the Commanding Officer just had to indicate which plan had to be followed.'

At the same time the Norfolks' Corps Commander, Lieutenant General Barker was showing signs of severe stress. Lieutenant General Brooke found him 'in a very difficult state to deal with, he is so overwrought with work and the present situation that he sees dangers where they don't exist and cannot make up his mind on any points. He is quite impossible to cooperate with. He has been worse than ever today [18 May] and whenever anything is fixed he changes his mind shortly afterwards.'[8]

Unfortunately, Barker grew steadily worse. During the last days of the evacuation, when Gort nominated him to command the remainder of the BEF, Barker, on leaving the meeting, questioned why the responsibility had been thrust onto him. Although not said directly to Gort, the British Commander-in-Chief must have harboured enough doubts to appoint Major General Alexander instead. Montgomery regarded Barker as 'an utterly useless commander who had lost his nerve by 30th May' – a typically outspoken assessment of a man who, sadly, was to suffer a nervous breakdown.

Reconnaissance of defensive positions along the west bank of the River Dendre commenced at approximately 0600 on 18 May. The Brigade was to cover the sector between Grammont and Lessines [Lessen] with two battalions forward – Norfolks on the left, Royal Scots on the right – and the Lancashire Fusiliers in reserve. By 0900, the Holy Boys had taken up their positions south of Grammont while Battalion HQ remained at Ribstraat.

Although there was a great deal of German air activity over Grammont, the Norfolks' sector remained relatively quiet. At around midday, bridges spanning the Dendre were blown and outposts on the eastern side, who had been skirmishing with German units, were withdrawn during the afternoon. With the bridges destroyed, some of the men thought that the river presented a formidable obstacle and certainly the Germans made no imme- diate attempt to cross. Instead, they regrouped and prepared. Then, with darkness falling, the crossing began utilizing rubber dinghies and barges; some even swam across. But as the Germans began to establish themselves on the western bank, the Norfolks received orders at 0100 hrs on 19 May for a further withdrawal to

Froidment on the River Escaut. Barclay explained:

> We never ever carried out a withdrawal in contact. If we
> thought that was likely, we patrolled very offensively against
> the enemy positions before we pulled out; gave them some-
> thing to think about and then extricated ourselves without
> fear of interference. This, in fact, occurred every time; we were
> never once molested in our withdrawal which I was thankful
> about because nearly always I was a rearguard company and
> you had a horrible sort of feeling of getting one up the pants
> as you were coming out. But it never came to that.

Despite the shortage of transport enough was eventually found
to lift each battalion in turn. The Norfolks met theirs at 0400 near
the village of Ronse (Renaix) after a march of around 12 miles. The
rearguard, following behind, commandeered some Royal Army
Service Corps lorries in the same village. Progress was slow, with
roads particularly near towns and villages heavily congested.
German aircraft swept in adding death and destruction to the chaos
below. In one instance five planes destroyed three of the Norfolks'
vehicles, including an ammunition truck, causing several casualties.

As the men scattered, Private Albert Pooley dived into a ploughed
field where he tried to conceal himself in a furrow. One of the
German aeroplanes must have noticed him for 'he saw a red light
winking in the tail – not until bullets spattered all round him did
he realize the significance of the light.'[9]

Between the Holy Boys and their objective Froidmont, lay the
town of Tournai (Doornik) which, according to the Norfolks' War
Diary 'was being heavily bombed from the air and was being
rapidly demolished as the Bn approached.' As there were no guides
and 'a great shortage of maps', confusion reigned; the pace of the
withdrawal slowed even more while the Battalion tried to find
alternative routes via secondary roads. 'Efforts to control the
column,' according to the Regimental History, 'resulted in different
orders being issued, so that vehicles became widely scattered, and
many lost their way and did not join the battalion until evening.'

Pooley was extremely lucky to rejoin the battalion at all. He took
his truck through the burning town and just managed to slam on
the brakes when a high wall bulged and then collapsed across the

road in front of him. The roar of falling masonry was deafening and his truck was covered by a layer of dust.[10]

By the day's end, Froidment had been reached. 'Billeting area in Chateau grounds,' wrote Captain Long. 'All troops under cover in woods – slit trenches dug against an attack . . . Bn strength showed many missing.'

A quiet night enabled the exhausted men to get their heads down and try to catch up on sleep. The following morning was spent resting and cleaning. Tournai was still under heavy aerial attack and some artillery shells were fired on Froidment but luckily no casualties were suffered. A reconnaissance of the river was carried out between Tournai and Antoing.

Later that afternoon, as the Holy Boys were about to have tea, they were 'suddenly ordered out to arrest or shoot the villagers who had refused to evacuate and were beginning to demonstrate. So far as can be ascertained order was restored. These civilians may have been Germans in disguise.' This is how the incident is described in the Battalion's War Diary which, owing to the original being destroyed, was compiled some years later. The War Diary of 4th Infantry Brigade is, however, more specific. It records:

> At 1600 hrs a report was received that 70 civilians had crossed the river at Calonne and had barricaded themselves into some houses and fired on anyone approaching. 2n Bn RNR were ordered forward at short notice to check any further infiltration if necessary and with this in view, they marched out of Froidment and took up position of assembly in a wood behind St Maur.

Captain Long refers to the incident as 'rioting by 5th Columnists' but made no other comment only to say that the orders were cancelled.

Stories of German parachutists and fifth column activities were legion in those nerve-racking times. Five days before, while on the Dyle, a contingent of Holy Boys had been sent to investigate reports of a German parachute landing. They found nothing, but the conclusion was that it was evident 'the rumours had fifth column sources to cause confusion.' Allied soldiers chased shadows of rumour and, with increasing paranoia about German infiltration, innocent civilians became spies. Many were summarily executed simply because they looked or behaved suspiciously. The French, British and Belgians must all bear responsibility for such acts.

After their fruitless search for fifth columnists, the Norfolks moved forward from St Maur to the banks of the River Escaut. Shortly before midnight the Brigade was in position with all three battalions in the line: Royal Scots on the right, Lancashire Fusiliers in the centre, and Holy Boys on the left. The War Diary of 4 Brigade states that the Norfolks were at Chateau de Coucou. No longer was the Brigade on the extreme right of the BEF front: there were now three – 5th, 144th and 145th brigades – between them and the junction with the French.

Seven British divisions were to defend a line of 32 miles, from north of Oudenaarde southwards to Maulde on the Franco-Belgian frontier. Nearly all brigades were forward with a thin reserve consisting of the 133rd, 12th, 6th and 143rd brigades. Defensive depth appears to have been sacrificed for concentration on the river line itself. 'On average each battalion in a forward position was to be responsible for something like a mile of winding river bank.'

This, of course, meant that the frontage covered by individual companies would also be long: 'about 700 or 800 yards, which was a lot for a company in close country,' said Peter Barclay. 'A' Company had taken over positions near Cherq from the Royal Berkshire Regiment and the men were proceeding to strengthen them.

> There were buildings on our side of the canal and there was a plantation on the enemy side so we had to have a pretty effective system of cross fire. My company preparations were completed during the hours of darkness. I went round and they were jolly well camouflaged too. Some were in the cellars with sort of loopholes just under the roofs, one lot hiding behind a garden wall with loopholes; well concealed positions which gave good coverage of the frontage I was responsible for.

One building occupied by a section from Barclay's company was a former cement factory. 'The roof was off it,' recalled Ernie Leggett, 'but we were able to get up on a veranda on the second floor, fairly high. We got what wood and material we could. We just shoved it up so that we were covered to a certain extent. We were very much concealed.'

'A' Company was in the centre of the battalion line with 'D' to the left, 'B' on the right and 'C' in reserve. Battalion HQ was established in a large Chateau in Calonne. Although the company and platoon positions were sited so as to be mutually supporting, there were inevitably blind spots on such a wide front, through which the Germans would be able to penetrate, especially in dark or misty conditions. To add to the problems, the Escaut was becoming less of an obstacle, with the water dropping to a dangerously low level, 'at places less than three feet deep,' according to Lord Gort. 'It looked, therefore, as if apart from the unusually dry weather, some of the sluices in the neighbourhood of Valenciennes had been closed in order to produce inundations in the low lying ground in that area – even if at the expense of the water on the front of the BEF.'

During the trek back from the Dyle, morale among the Holy Boys had remained high. They were ready and willing to take on the Germans. 'Why can't we fight it out? Why can't we stand and have it out with them?' were the constant questions asked by the rank and file. Now, it seemed, they were going to be given their chance. Brigadier Warren, commander of 4th Infantry Brigade, was informed late on the 20th that it was the BEF's intention to 'stand and fight' on this position.

The overall picture was bleak, however. Guderian's Panzers had reached Abbeville and one of his forward units was already on the Channel coast. The final entry on 20 May in the War Diary of Army Group A read: 'Now that we have reached the coast at Abbeville the first stage of the offensive has been achieved . . . The possibility of an encirclement of the Allied armies' northern group is beginning to take shape.' They would soon be in a position to move north-east along the coast to Boulogne, Calais and Dunkirk.

In the early hours of Tuesday, 21 May, Captain Barclay was hunting but his quarry on this occasion was black rabbits, not Germans. His batman had noticed the creatures in the grounds of the chateau where some of his company's positions were located. Barclay recalled:

And not only that, but he'd also found some ferrets in a box in the stables. I'm ashamed to say, there were also a couple of retrievers kept shut up in the stables; all the occupants of the chateau and everybody else round about had departed, except in a little convent nearby where two nuns had remained. So we thought we'd get in a bit of sport before the fun began.

I had a shotgun with me and we popped these ferrets down a big warren and we were having a bit of sport as rabbits bolted out of these burrows, when after about an hour and a half of this, shelling started along the river line generally. And we came in for a certain amount of this and we thought: 'Well, we'd better pack this up now and deal with the other situation.' So back we went to Company Headquarters and waited for the next pattern of activities.

The Brigade War Diary records that the German attack commenced at '0440 hrs; the SOS was fired by the right Coy ['B' Company] of 2nd Bn The Royal Norfolk Regiment and artillery fire was immediately brought to bear. The enemy used shrapnel and mortar fire very effectively and followed this up with intense M.G. fire.'

Battalion HQ at Calonne was shelled and when a mortar round struck the porch, three officers were wounded: Major Charlton, Major Marshall the Adjutant and Second-Lieutenant Buckingham, all were successfully evacuated. The 37-seven-year-old Major Lisle Ryder assumed command, with Captain Charles Long as Adjutant. No Second in Command was appointed for the time being. Captain Gordon became OC HQ Company in addition to his duties as Signals Officer.

When Germans began to appear on the opposite bank, Captain Barclay decided not to engage them immediately and ordered his men to hold their fire until they heard his hunting horn.

Unaware that they were being watched, a German officer, surrounded by some of his senior warrant officers, stood in full view studying a map. The Holy Boys, well concealed in their trenches and buildings, waited while young trees were cut from the plantation to make hurdles for crossing the river. They allowed the Germans to position the trees across the remains of a demolished bridge and start to scramble over. When around twenty-five were across and others were grouping on the far bank ready to mount the makeshift bridge, Barclay's hunting horn rasped out. His men opened fire:

> with consummate accuracy and disposed of all the enemy personnel on our side of the canal and also the ones on the bank at the far side . . . then, of course, we came in for an inordinate amount of shelling and mortar fire. After the initial burst of fire and their enormous casualties they knew pretty well where we were. Their mortar fire was very accurate. Not so long after, I was wounded in the guts, back and arm. I had a field dressing put on each of my wounds.

As there had been several casualties, no stretcher-bearers were immediately available for Barclay, but his ever-resourceful batman:

> with great presence of mind, ripped a door off its hinges and in spite of my orders to the contrary, tied me on to this door. In fact, had he not done this I probably wouldn't be here to tell the tale. But there I was tied to this door and I thought: 'Right, well now, you've got to take me round on this door because you've not only got my weight to contend with but you've got the door as well.' And so, of course, that took four people.

Opposing the Holy Boys was the 2nd Battalion Infantry Regiment 54 of the 18th Infantry Division,[11] who displayed a reckless determination to break the defenders. In the face of heavy fire from the Norfolks, they attacked in what Tim Carew described as 'closely packed masses reminiscent of Mons in 1914 . . . seemingly heedless of casualties.'[12] The Germans themselves later admitted in the Official History of the 18th Infantry Division that owing to previous successes they were becoming overconfident.

Elements from the 2nd Battalion Infantry Regiment 54 eventually succeeded in gaining a foothold, forcing the line between the Norfolks and Lancashire Fusiliers. 'B' Company's positions were overrun exposing 'A' Company's right flank.

'Suddenly,' said Barclay, who was still commanding from his

makeshift stretcher, 'we were fired at by Germans from our side of the canal.'

To deal with this dangerous development, Company Sergeant Major George Gristock assembled a party of eight men, including a company clerk and a wireless operator, from Company HQ. According to the Regimental History:

> He realized that an enemy machine-gun had been brought up to a position where it was causing severe casualties in the company and went forward by himself, with one man as connecting file, to try and put it out of action. He himself came under heavy machine-gun fire from another position and was severely wounded in both legs [his right knee was badly smashed]. He dragged himself forward to within twenty yards of the enemy gun and, by well-directed fire, killed the crew of four and put the gun out of action. He then made his way back to the company flank and directed the defence, refusing to be evacuated until contact with the battalion on the right had been made and the line restored.

At this point 'C' Company arrived and consolidated the right flank, but they now had to take over the position formerly occupied by 'B' Company which left the Battalion without a reserve.

Later, Barclay and Gristock, together with Captain Allen of 'B' Company were evacuated. Lieutenant Yallop assumed command of 'A' Company and Lieutenant Edgeworth 'B' Company.

Another to be evacuated was Ernie Leggett. From his elevated position about 100 yards away, on the cement factory veranda, he had watched the heroism of what he described as 'a solitary figure' dealing with the machine-gun posts. Before being severely wounded, Leggett helped repulse further German attacks. He vividly recalled the sheer recklessness of them:

> We saw the Germans coming at us through the wood and they also had light tanks. We let them have all we'd got, firing the Bren, rifles and everything. I was on the Bren gun firing from the cover of these old benches, tables and God knows what on the veranda. We killed a lot of Germans. They came up almost as far as the river and we really gave them hell and they

retreated. They attacked us again and the tanks were coming over their own dead men. To us, that was repulsive and we couldn't understand why they did that. We put them back again, we just fired at them – they weren't the heavy tanks. There was no bridge near me so they couldn't get across the river. We managed to keep them on their side. They attacked us three times and three times we sent them back.

We were being shelled by their artillery, but the mortars were the things which were causing the damage. It was terrible, just terrible! You can more or less hear the thing sort of pump off and the next thing you know there's an explosion. Out of my section [about eight to ten men] in the end was myself, two other privates and a Lance Corporal.

It was a mortar blast that almost accounted for Ernie Leggett. He was flung into the air and when he came down he felt numb from the waist down, and couldn't move his legs. Blood was oozing from a gaping wound in his groin where a jagged shell fragment over three inches long and about an inch and a half wide had passed completely through him, entering his left buttock and exiting through the groin.

My pals, they got their and my dressings, we only had one each. It was no good just tying them round, it was insufficient. So they bunged one into the wound at the back, pushed it up, put another into the wound at the front and they tied the other two outside. Then they got a piece of rope and tied a tourniquet. I was bleeding a lot. Fortunately, I was numb. I had no pain, that's the amazing thing about it.

Having been carried down the stairs, he was left to his own devices as his mates were duty bound to return to their positions. Slowly, he started to drag himself in the direction of his Company's HQ following a railway line.

I crawled and crawled. They'd taken my trousers off; all I'd got was a rough pair of pants and battledress top. Meantime, they were bombing us from above. I was being covered with earth, everything and God knows what.

As I was crawling along I was conscious that my fingernails had been worn down so that they were bleeding; my hands were bleeding . . . It was determination to get away, like a wounded animal. It took me ages. It was about a hundred, hundred and twenty yards from our headquarters; I was almost at my last gasp, and there was one hell of an explosion and I was covered with earth, and I said, 'Please, God, help me.'

I don't know how long I was out but I then remember my hands and arms being tugged and I heard someone say, 'Bloody hell, it's Ernie!'

I looked up into the faces of two bandsmen. They take on the job of stretcher bearers: Lance Corporal John Woodrow and a chap named 'Bunt' Bonham. They pulled me out and I heard them talking: 'Bloody hell, he's had it!'

Attacks continued into the night and again there was a breakthrough. The Lancashire Fusiliers were reported to be wheeling backwards exposing the Norfolks' right flank. Lieutenant Woodwark of 'C' Company was ordered back to Battalion HQ to update them on the situation. Brigade was informed and a company from the 1st Royal Welch Fusiliers from 6 Brigade was brought up to cover the increasing gap. In the meantime, 'C' Company successfully repulsed the attack.

As the night wore on, the gunfire died down but never ceased. At dawn on 22 May, the heavy German attacks resumed all along the British front. Attempts were made to cross the canal by way of ruined bridges and some tried to swim across, but the line held. The British suffered casualties but the Germans were paying a higher price for their reckless courage. During the previous day's fighting, for example, the 18th Infantry Division had suffered a total of 544 casualties: 5 officers, 19 NCOs and 107 men killed; 15 officers, 51 NCOs and 339 wounded; 8 men were posted as missing. The commander of the 2nd Battalion Infantry Regiment 54, Major Lengerke, was amongst those killed.[13]

Bob Brown described the carnage in front of 'A' Company's position. He had been detailed to run a message to the company where one of his fellow signallers was doing infantry duty at the time. 'He called me over and told me to look forward from the position. And all I could see was rows and rows and rows of German dead – about three hundred yards away. He said they'd been coming over in mass formation and the Bren-gunners were firing straight ahead and they just couldn't miss them . . . they were just determined to get forward at any expense.'

Inevitably, with such a wide front, further German penetrations were made. A sniper succeeded in gaining a position to the rear of the Holy Boys' Battalion HQ, rendering all movement in that vicinity extremely dangerous with his accurate fire. Second Lieutenant Willeson led a patrol to try and flush him out but was unsuccessful.

Civilian movement in the area also added to the problems, resulting in several innocent people being accidentally shot by both sides. Albert Pooley witnessed such an incident when three French civilians – an old man, a woman, and a young woman – came along the road in front of his position which was concealed behind one of the chateau's perimeter walls. Pooley shouted a warning to his fellow Norfolks but suddenly the Frenchman collapsed and one of the women screamed. Whether they had been shot by the Germans on the other side of the water, or by one of the Company, Pooley did not know, but he left his post and with the help of two or three others managed to get the two wounded and the young woman into shelter. The man had a very serious wound and the woman was badly hit in the face. Pooley learnt later that she recovered but the man died before he could be got to hospital.[14]

At 1700 hrs that afternoon, 4th Infantry Brigade HQ received orders that despite the 'stand and fight' message, 2nd Division was to withdraw to the Gort Line. 'Troops could not understand,' commented the Brigade's War Diary, 'why they could not stand and fight on the good obstacles. There was a feeling that the British Army was running away.'

Gort and his three corps commanders, Michael Barker, Alan Brooke and Sir Ronald Adam, had decided that a further retirement was necessary during a meeting held twenty-four hours previously. With water levels in the Escaut so low that it no longer formed an effective tank obstacle, and with British troops spread somewhat thinly across the front, a prolonged defence was impossible. Gort believed that by retreating to the well-prepared defences along the frontier between Belgium and France 'advantage could be taken of the existing blockhouses and trenches, and of the anti-tank ditch'.

The British, however, could not make such a decision unilaterally; agreement had to be sought with their Allies. By 2000 on 21 May, Gort was in Ypres where he belatedly joined a conference of Allied commanders, which had been going on for much of the day. He was unable to see the new Commander-in-Chief of the Allied forces, General Weygand, who had replaced Gamelin on 20 May, because he had left Ypres before Gort arrived. Gort, however, did meet the Belgian King, Leopold III, and General Billotte to whom he was able to explain the situation developing on the Escaut front. 'It was thereupon decided,' wrote Gort, 'that the Escaut should be abandoned on the night of 22nd–23rd May and the line be withdrawn to the Belgian frontier defences.'

Covered by the Norfolks' Carrier Platoon under Second Lieutenant Elson, and supplemented by carriers of the 4th/7th Royal Dragoon Guards, the Holy Boys withdrew from their positions and set off on foot for the Bois de Wannehain. The distance, as the crow flies, is some 8 miles but the march took them nine hours. Detours caused by severe bomb damage to the roads ensured another two hours of marching before they reached their objective at 1100 hrs. The War Diary of 4th Infantry Brigade said that the Norfolks and Lancashire Fusiliers manned blockhouses on the Gort Line which had been built by the 1st Division: Bachy, Hellfire Corner and Bourghelles.

'Route back,' concluded the entry, 'took Bde to within 3 miles from where it had started 12 days before – a withdrawal of 64 miles having been completed in 6 days.'

By this time Captain Barclay was on his way to the coast and Blighty. He later described his evacuation as 'a pretty hair-raising time'. From the battlefield he had been taken to the Regimental First Aid Post where both he and Company Sergeant Major Gristock, who was in a very bad state, enjoyed some jellified brandy pills. 'They were delicious and very welcoming' and cheered up Gristock no end.

Barclay was then taken to a 'larger medical rendezvous' where he remembered arriving but nothing of the journey. With him was the little Belgian dog, the black mongrel bitch, which would not leave his side.

She was lying on top of me preventing anybody getting anywhere near me. And then they cut off my trousers . . . mutilated them . . . which I thought was a most awful waste of a reasonable pair of battledress trousers. My little dog was so concerned about this that they had to put a bag over her and take her away and I never saw her anymore. It was too awful.

Anyhow, then four of us were put into an improvised small bus. It was a sort of tradesman's van really. We were evacuated in this and we'd gone some little distance when the driver brought the vehicle to a very abrupt halt and turned round unceremoniously in the road. It had an open back, this thing, and there we were looking out of the back and there, about twenty yards away, was a German tank sitting in the middle of the road. However, we had a red cross painted on the side and the chap forbore to fire at us and on our way we went until we eventually finished up at a station and this sort of hospital train. They were all stretcher cases on this hospital train.

Barclay thought that the train first took them to Dunkirk, but as there was no hospital ship expected at the port, the train went to Boulogne. Again there was no hospital ship and so they were shunted the few miles to Calais.

He recalled the scene at the quay where Thames barges were drawing alongside, unloading Bren-gun carriers which were immediately manned and driven off to confront the Germans.

A hospital ship was due in at Calais that night but as the quay was a ready target for German dive-bombers, the train was shunted away to an area which Barclay described as no man's land.

'This was a most eerie feeling,' he recounted. 'We were on an embankment with obviously our Red Cross designations very conspicuous all over the train. And there we were, with the German forces on one side and our own forces on the other. We could only really tell this from the explosions that were going on either side, and none going on where we were.'

After dark, the train moved down to the mole and transfer to the hospital ship commenced.

'We'd been in the hospital train for four days and there were only dressings available for twenty-four hours. So therefore people couldn't be re-dressed and a lot of the wounded were suffering terribly from gangrene and the smell was appalling.'

Barclay went on to pay a warm tribute to the team of doctors and nurses on the train, who he believed were all Territorials. 'Everybody felt full of admiration for them and the work they did under such adverse conditions.'

The medical team was ordered on to the ship although the ship itself had a full complement of medics. But the Territorials refused to obey. They said that they were going to stay with the defenders of Calais and continue working for the wounded in France. Not one of them embarked.

In the early hours of the following morning the ship arrived in Newhaven. Barclay said that he experienced the most extra-ordinary anti-climax. He had become acclimatized to the appalling din of the battlefield and then came the peace of Britain – dead silence except for the odd seagull.

After disembarkation, the officers were sent to Ashridge Park in Berkshire and the other ranks to Hatfield Park, which proved to be an administrative cock-up.

'Hatfield Park,' as Barclay pointed out, 'was laid out for officers, with small rooms of two or three beds in each room, and Ashridge Park was laid out for other ranks. However, they tried to move us after we got there but we wouldn't be shifted in spite of rather dictatorial matrons.'

Notes

1. Churchill, W.S., *The Second World War*, vol. II, *Their Finest Hour*, Cassell, 1959.
2. *Ibid.*
3. Mellenthin, *Panzer Battles*.
4   Caddick-Adams, Peter, 'The German Breakthrough at Sedan, 12–15 May 1940', from *The Battle for France and Flanders Sixty Years On*, Professor Brian Bond and Michael Taylor (eds), Leo Cooper, 2001.
5. Jackson, *The Fall Of France*, from p. 32, by permission of Oxford University Press.
6. Caddick-Adams, 'The German Breakthrough'.
7. Sebag-Montefiore, *Dunkirk*, Hastings.
8. Alanbrooke, *War Diaries*, diary entry for 18 May 1940.
9. Jolly, *The Vengeance of Private Pooley*.
10. *Ibid.*

11. Sarkar, *Guards VC.*
12. Carew, Tim, *The Royal Norfolk Regiment*, Royal Norfolk Regiment Association, 1991; reproduced by kind permission of the Trustees of the Royal Norfolk Regimental Museum, Norwich.
13. Sarkar, *Guards VC.*
14. Jolly, *The Vengeance of Private Pooley.*

CHAPTER 6

'The Führer is beside himself with joy.'

As early as 19 May, Lord Gort's Chief of Staff, Lieutenant General Pownall, had telephoned the War Office in London to discuss the possibility of a withdrawal to the Channel Ports, or even from the Continent of Europe itself. Although, at this stage, lines of communication had not been severed – rail and road links across the River Somme at Abbeville were still intact – it would only be a matter of time before the German Panzers cut this last tenuous link. The Allied forces in the north-east would be isolated – the French from their armies in the south and the British from their western rearward areas. 'The picture,' wrote Gort, 'was no longer of a line bent or broken, but of a besieged fortress.'

Later that day, a meeting was held in the War Office at which Bertram Ramsay, Vice Admiral Dover, was present. Maintaining a temporary supply line to the BEF and the evacuation of some personnel through the ports of Boulogne, Calais and Dunkirk was discussed. The question of a major evacuation of forces was also considered. But London, it seems, knew little about the true military situation in France that it regarded such a measure as unlikely, although 'seven days later it developed into Operation "Dynamo".' According to Vice Admiral Ramsey, 'the main decision . . . was that the control must be delegated to the Vice Admiral Dover, and available shipping placed at his disposal.'[1]

Despite such contingency plans, the British Cabinet was against withdrawal and 'decided that the BEF must fight its way southwards towards Amiens to make contact with the French.'[2] Churchill was still undoubtedly expecting the counter-attack he had demanded of General Gamelin during a Supreme War Council meeting in Paris on 16 May. Gamelin had indeed drafted an order

95

for an attack on the Germans flanks – in fact, his only order since fighting began. On 20 May, however, he was sacked by Reynaud and replaced by 73-year-old General Maxime Weygand, who flew in from Syria to take up his appointment. Before confirming an order issued by his predecessor, Weygand had to familiarize himself with the situation. Gamelin's order was cancelled the next day, 21 May.

Chief of the Imperial General Staff, Sir Edmund Ironside, travelled to France on 20 May to convey the British Cabinet's orders to Gort. Gort told him that an attack towards Amiens would be impracticable as seven divisions would have to be detached from the Escaut front where the BEF was already heavily engaged. Any weakening of that sector would be quickly exploited by the enemy. He planned to use his only available reserves for an advance on Arras, where they would relieve the town's garrison which was in danger of being completely encircled.

A major attack like that ordered by the British Cabinet would also require considerable input from the French, but British commanders were rapidly losing faith in their ally. Billotte, in particular, as coordinator of the Allied forces, was causing great concern – he appeared to have become mentally paralysed by the German breakthrough. Morale at his HQ had hit the floor and looked as if it was going to stay there indefinitely. Lack of communication was also a source of friction. Gort had not received any orders directly from Billotte for eight days, but it has to be said that Gort should bear some responsibility for allowing such a situation to occur. He could at least have complained to the British Cabinet.

An attempt was now made by the British to strengthen the projected Arras operation and bring it as near conformity to Cabinet orders as possible. To seek French involvement, Ironside and Pownall went straight to Billotte's HQ at Lens, where they found Billotte and Blanchard 'in a state of depression' as Ironside put it. 'No plan, no thought of a plan. Ready to be slaughtered.'[3]

Pownall said that 'they were in a proper dither, even Blanchard who is not *nerveux*. But the two of them and [Colonel] Alembert were all three shouting at one moment – Billotte shouted loudest, trembling, that he had no means to deal with tanks and that if his infantry were put into line they would not withstand attack.'[4]

Ironside admitted to losing his temper with his much shorter

French counterpart. In the usual British way, Ironside, whose 6 foot 4 inches and broad build gave him a commanding presence, had acquired the nickname 'Tiny'. Looming over Gaston Billotte, he shook him 'by the button of his tunic'.[5]

During these heated exchanges, Gort telephoned to inform them that he was putting the 5th and 50th divisions into the Arras attack, which was to commence the following day. Ironside and Pownall managed to get Billotte's agreement to send two divisions southwards from Douai towards Cambrai and for elements of General Prioux's 3 DLM to cooperate on the British right.

'This is our last reserve,' said Pownall. 'We cannot do much more in the common cause.'[6]

That evening, 2nd Panzer Division was at Abbeville, still some 10 miles short of the coast. An Austrian battalion made up the deficit by moving on to Noyelles-sur-Mer. Hitler, anxious at the risks his armoured units had been taking and who had railed against their recklessness, was overcome at the news that the Channel had been reached.

'The Führer is beside himself with joy,' General Jodl, the *Wehrmacht*'s operations chief, confided to his diary. 'Talks in words of the highest appreciation of the German army and its leadership. Is working on a peace treaty.' But events that began to unfold the following day created alarm once again about the vulnerability of the Panzer corridor.

Notwithstanding the lack of French support, the British went ahead with the Arras operation on the afternoon of 21 May. Commanded by Major General Franklyn, the original concept of two divisions was reduced to two battalions: the 6th and 8th Durham Light Infantry, with a third battalion, the 9th, following in reserve. The force also consisted of assorted anti-tank units,[7] motorcycle scouts and seventy-four tanks. Tank numbers had been reduced through mechanical breakdown and many of those which did take part were in bad need of overhaul.

Supported by elements of 3 DLM, the force split into two columns which moved west of Arras. When the columns made contact with the Germans – SS Infantry and Rommel's Panzers – 'Frankforce' as the formation was known, punched well above its weight. Rommel, normally the coolest of commanders, was alarmed and in a subsequent report stated that there were 'hundreds of enemy tanks' and 'five enemy divisions.' He eventually managed to restore the situation but lost more tanks that day than in any previous operation. The German War Diary puts casualties at 378.

For such a small ad hoc formation, 'Frankforce' demonstrated what a much larger force might have been able to achieve against the stretched German lines. Lord Gort, however, knew that although his objective had been reached, 'Frankforce' could not maintain its momentum, unless reinforced by those French divisions that Billotte had supposedly agreed to send.

While the British were busy denting the pride of the SS and 7th Panzer Division, General Weygand was in Ypres at a conference of senior field commanders, outlining his plan for a major counter-attack. As mentioned in the previous chapter, Gort arrived too late to speak to Weygand. His discussions with Billotte and the Belgian King were primarily about withdrawal from the Escaut to the 'Gort Line'. Unfortunately, Billotte was seriously injured when his car crashed while motoring back to his HQ. His death two days later left the Allied armies without a co-ordinator until replaced by Blanchard, 'who seemed even more overwhelmed by events than Billotte had been. "Pretty wet" was Pownall's verdict.'[8]

Weygand's plan, as outlined by General Hastings Ismay, Churchill's staff officer, 'was that the French First Army and the BEF should attack south-west, while a new French Army Group that was now being formed from here, there and everywhere, under command of General Frère, was to attack northwards from south of the Somme and join hands with them'.[9] The earliest date for the attack would be 26 May.

In order to free sufficient divisions for the northern part of the operation, the Allied line in the east would have to be shortened and held by the Belgians. At a meeting with Churchill and Reynaud in Paris on 22 May, Weygand claimed that the southern army's strength was between eighteen and twenty divisions.

Churchill had been advocating a concerted attack on the fragile Panzer corridor all along, to cut off that metaphorical tortoise head. He was so impressed by Weygand's confidence and apparent fighting spirit that on returning to London, he sent a telegram to Gort ordering the BEF to take part. General Pownall was enraged: 'How is an attack like this to be staged involving three nationalities at an hour's notice? The man's mad. I suppose these figments of the imagination are telegraphed without consulting his military advisers.'[10]

In truth, they were not figments of the Prime Minister's imagination. He had taken Weygand and the plan at face value. What he did not know was that Frère's army was only around six divisions strong, 65 miles away and moving very slowly.

London, however, was aware that the situation was deteriorating. When Churchill telephoned Paris on 23 May, he was reassured that Frère's forces had taken Amiens. This was palpably untrue. But on the same day, the War Minister, Anthony Eden, gave assurances that naval and air arrangements would be in place if the BEF had to withdraw to the coast.

'Tiny' Ironside considered that Weygand's plan would have been ideal

> if it had been issued and acted on earlier . . . it would certainly be too late by the time subordinate commanders had given their orders and positioned their troops. The gap between the German armour and its supporting formations was gradually closing. Bombing delayed the arrival of the French Army Group in the south. Nearly the whole of the BEF was in contact with the enemy and would be difficult to disengage, while Billotte . . . the only Frenchman who knew of Weygand's Plan was dead. No successor was appointed for some days and orders arrived late.[11]

Increasing enemy pressure on Arras compelled Gort to order the withdrawal of his forces there on the evening of 23 May. 'Thus concluded the defence of Arras,' he wrote, 'which had been carried out by a small garrison, hastily assembled but well commanded, and determined to fight. It had imposed a valuable delay on a greatly superior force against which it had blocked a vital road centre.'

As 'Frankforce' pulled out, heading in a north-easterly direction, suspicions regarding British intentions arose amongst the French. It was suggested that Gort was abandoning his role in Weygand's counter-attack and was marching north with the intention of evacuating his army. Paris informed London that because of Gort's action the plan would have to be altered. Churchill argued that he knew nothing about a retreat and reiterated his commitment to the Weygand Plan. But the French would not be pacified and their suspicions grew. The 16-mile withdrawal was soon exaggerated to a 25-mile retreat to the Channel Ports. Such were the recriminations that it seemed as though Weygand himself was looking for excuses to ditch his much-vaunted plan – because of lack of troops, tanks and aircraft – and was using the British movements as the way out.

Although sceptical, Gort was still prepared to play his part. Two divisions, or at least the remnants of the 5th and 50th were available. He considered that the main weight of thrust must come from Frère's army gathering in the south. The French, in response, accused Gort of trying to shift responsibility for the attack.

Gort was well aware that his troops were battle weary and that pressure was mounting from Army Group B in the east. In II Corps' sector, Lieutenant General Brooke received a report on 24 May that the Germans had penetrated the Belgian line between Coutrai and Menin exposing the flank of his corps. Despite making temporary adjustments, he needed reinforcements quickly and felt that by holding back his reserve divisions in readiness for the counter-attack, Gort was failing to recognize the threat to the eastern line. On 25 May, without consulting either the French or the War Cabinet in London, Gort dispatched his reserves to assist Brooke – a move that finally killed off the counter-offensive.

Two days earlier, Brooke had written in his diary: 'Nothing but a miracle can save the BEF now and the end cannot be very far off.'[12] The end was less than a fortnight away but the Allies were now given a chink of time through which a large part of the trapped army could squeeze. In hindsight, what to the Germans was an operational decision could be construed as a minor miracle for the BEF. However, that miracle still came at a high price for those units which remained behind to fight to the last so that others might escape.

On 24 May, the German Panzers were halted on 'the Führer's orders'. Much to the fury of officers like Guderian, the tanks remained 'rooted to the ground' for two days with advanced units just 10 miles from the port of Dunkirk. Initially, the decision was von Rundstedt's, who was very apprehensive about the vulnerability of the Panzer corridor. Arras had provided a demonstration of its fragility. It had to be strengthened by allowing the infantry and other support units to catch up and consolidate the ground already taken. There was also the fear that the Panzers would become bogged down in the terrain around Dunkirk. Also the tanks themselves were in need of mechanical overhaul for there was still a lot of fighting to do. Once the campaign in the north-east was finished a new operation had to be mounted against those armies which remained intact south and west of the German lines.

When Hitler visited von Rundstedt at the HQ of Army Group A at 1130 hrs on the morning of 24 May, the Führer, who shared his general's nervousness about the speed of advance, ratified the decision to halt. In the meantime, the Luftwaffe could play a major offensive role, something that Göring, its Commander-in-Chief, had wanted badly while enviously watching the Panzers' startling success. He assured Hitler that his pilots would do the job. So the *Haltbefehl* directive was issued: 'By the Führer's orders . . . the general line Lens–Béthune–St Omer–Gravelines will <u>not</u> be passed.'

In recent years the distinguished German historian, Lieutenant Colonel Dr Karl-Heinz Frieser, has offered another view of this controversial order. That Hitler's ratification 'was as much an attempt to reimpose, in a bizarre way, his authority over his generals (almost out of spite) and to regain control over the campaign which had run away on its own, as it was to respond to the perceived threat to his exposed flanks, a danger underlined by the Arras counter attack.'[13]

Gravelines (on the coast), St Omer, Aire, Béthune, La Bassée – the Canal Line; these places were all linked by a continuous line of canals and canalized rivers providing an artery for trade. Now this same system of waterways had to be utilized as an anti-tank ditch, a natural defensive barrier to protect the southern and western flanks of the Allied Armies. The Gort Line in the east had been worked on extensively during the 'Phoney War' to defend against what was thought to be the major route of attack. The break-through on the Meuse and subsequent rapid advance to the Channel had exposed the Allied flanks. Gort was now forced to improvise. The Canal Line would have to be defended, initially by such troops as could be found who could at least fire a rifle, until the eastern line was shortened and divisions freed to bolster these ad hoc measures.

A sector of the southern flank was already protected by a formation called 'Macforce'. Commanded by the BEF's former Director of Military Intelligence, Major General Mason-Macfarlane, it had begun life on 17 May and now had its HQ in the Royal Norfolks' old haunt of Orchies.

On 20 May, 'Polforce' (taking its name from the town of St Pol), under Major General Curtis, was created to continue the line on the right of 'Macforce' – from Pont Maudit to Aire. In Hazebrouck, Colonel Wood was organizing 'Woodforce' to provide a garrison for the town. Between Gravelines and St Mormelin, miscellaneous British troops were organized into 'Usherforce' under Colonel Usher.

By 23 May, the French First Army was able to take over the 'Macforce' sector. 'Macforce' itself, less one brigade which remained behind to come under the command of 'Polforce', moved to cover the line south of Hazebrouck in the Forêt de Nieppe.

Even when the French reinforced the line by taking over the northern sector near Gravelines, the defences were thinly spread. 'Macforce' had a battalion frontage of between 3 and 7 miles in width, impossible to defend. 'Polforce' was spread out over a distance of 40 miles. All these improvised formations could hope to do was cover the principal canal crossings until the other divisions arrived.

> The absence of any major attack on 24th enabled progress to be made in the adjustment of our forces which recent operations – and especially the development of a western front – had made urgently necessary. During the day GHQ issued an 'Operation Instruction' defining the changes to be made. This provided for the abolition of improvised forces, which could now be replaced by divisions freed from the eastern front.[14]

When the 'Operation Instruction' took effect on the morning of 25 May, the improvised forces were abolished.

The BEF had fallen back from the Escaut to the Gort Line during the night of 22/23 May and the defensive adjustments could be made. The 44th (Home Counties) Division was moved to the area south of Hazebrouck amalgamating with troops from 'Polforce'.

The 48th (South Midland) Division, less the 143 Brigade, was sent to strengthen strongpoints at Hazebrouck, Cassel, Wormhoudt and Bergues. The 2nd Division, plus 25 Brigade from 'Polforce', was to move into the Canal Line covering the front St Venant, Robecq and La Bassée. On their left, the area from La Bassée to Raches, was the responsibility of the 46th (North Midland and West Riding) Division which consisted only of 139 Brigade together with troops attached from other formations.

Things were fairly quiet for the Holy Boys on 23 May and they were able to rest in their positions on the Gort Line. At 1400 hrs that afternoon, a French Regiment of Zouavres started taking over the line and three hours later Divisional HQ issued orders for the Brigade to move into the area around Aubers which was about 20 miles to the west.

The Norfolks were relieved by the French in the evening but the *entente* was far from *cordiale*.

'They did not agree with the Gort Line positions,' wrote Murray Brown, 'and had spent the whole day digging a completely new defensive line. Throughout the day, parties and even individuals arrived at the position on bicycles and on foot and started digging.'

The move commenced at 2100 when 'C' Company embussed with the Royal Scots and the rest of the Battalion followed in Royal Army Service Corps transport. A thick curtain of mist and pitch darkness conspired to make the journey a slow and hazardous one.

At around 0700 the following morning, the CO, Major Ryder, and his party reached Aubers. Their billets, he was informed, were at Colon, around 8 miles further west, just north of Béthune. Captain Hastings was sent ahead to reconnoitre the sector.

'The new area was found to be the scene of terrible destruction,' recorded the Regimental History. 'Refugees massing the roads had been mown down by fighter attack and their bodies strewed the ground in hundreds. Almost every house had been destroyed and the war memorial, erected in memory of Indian troops who had given their lives in the 1914–18 war, had been demolished.'

Later that morning, between 1000 and 1100, the remainder of the Battalion under Major Richardson arrived at Colon after battling their way along heavily congested roads. As the men dispersed to their billets, they looked forward to a few days during which they could rest and refit. At least that is what their orders had led them to expect.

According to 4th Infantry Brigade HQ, there were no enemy troops near the area. French civilians, on the other hand, told a different tale. They were convinced that there were German units in the vicinity, but no definite intelligence could be obtained. The Luftwaffe was certainly very active and the Holy Boys paid great attention to the concealment of their positions.

With its strength reduced by the few days of hard fighting, 4th Infantry Brigade concentrated in the immediate area. In the southern part of Colon and the outskirts of Essars were the Royal Scots; a short distance to the north, Le Touret was occupied by the Lancashire Fusiliers. The Norfolks themselves were down to around half strength. Captain Long, in a return sent to Brigade HQ, numbered the battalion at 450, consisting of twenty-two officers and 428 other ranks.

The day or two of rest the Holy Boys had hoped for was soon reduced to a few hours. At 1400 that afternoon, Major Ryder received orders from Brigade to organize a reconnaissance of the La Bassée Canal (Canal d'Aire) from a bridge just outside Béthune to the Bois de Pacqueat. Ryder was told that he might have to take over this position because around 300 German infantry and a few AFVs had crossed the canal and engaged some French units.

Leaving Captain Nick Hallett in command of the battalion, Ryder set off an hour later, leading a party consisting of the Adjutant, the IO, the Signals Officer and all company commanders. Travelling in two cars, they made their way in a north-westerly direction along the canal from Béthune. Most of the journey was uneventful and no Germans or other Allied troops were encountered until they had almost reached the end of the sector. As they approached the village of Le Cornet Malo, a light machine-gun opened fire on the leading car containing Major Ryder. Captain Long wrote:

Range about 70 yards and figures of enemy clearly seen. One or two French Infantry were observed in action here. No other Allied troops noted. Cars were placed under cover & the recce attempted. Cars were sent off to RV at Locon. Continual fire from mortars, LMG & rifles was laid on the party & it was necessary to discontinue the effort. To get clear the party had to run and crawl in ditches for a considerable distance – fire was heavy from both sides of the Bois de Pacqueat. It was evident that enemy was over canal in several places.

Once clear of the danger area, Ryder decided to report personally to the Brigadier at l'Epinette. Unsure whether or not any other German units were in the area, he took the precaution of sending the Signals Officer ahead on a commandeered bicycle while the remainder followed on foot. According to Captain Long, Brigadier Warren 'did not appear to credit the information'; he believed the enemy to be across the canal in small numbers.

As they left Brigade HQ, German artillery opened fire, ranging between l'Epinette and Locon. Their journey on foot via l'Epinette must have taken several hours and by the time they reached the rendezvous point at Locon, the cars had returned to Colon.

When the weary party finally reached the battalion area, they found that their HQ and other buildings had been damaged by German artillery fire. Acting Major Elwes, said Captain Long in a detailed account of the battle of La Bassée Canal, 'had deployed the Bn into a defensive position facing towards Béthune having received information from returning French troops that enemy formations had forced the canal near Béthune & were advancing.'

Major Ryder and his officers held a short conference. It was a scene that Captain Hastings said he would never forget:

The room is lit by candles. The C.O. is so tired that his head keeps nodding as he talks, and he falls asleep. Charles Long is standing by his shoulder. We let him sleep for a minute. Then Charles taps the bottom of the candle on the table – gently – louder – louder still. The C.O. wakes up, and gets out a few more sentences, and goes off again. The same process is gone through again. It is repeated several times until the orders are complete. There is only one map. The heads of the company commanders are crowded round it. They are making what notes they can.[15]

From this one map of the area sketches were hastily made for each of the company commanders.

Through the gentle, lingering half light of dusk, the four companies, moving independently, set out to establish their positions covering the canal. At the same time Major Ryder had intended that Battalion HQ should move to the village of Le Paradis. Captain Hastings had been tasked with finding a suitable site, but driving in darkness, without lights, large-scale maps or signposts to guide him, he and his party eventually found themselves near Le Cornet Malo. They were forced to retrace their steps to Colon where it was decided that a temporary Battalion HQ should be set up near 'C' Company's HQ.[16]

Notes

1. Gardiner, W.J.R. (ed.), *The Evacuation from Dunkirk: Operation Dynamo 26 May–4 June 1940*, Naval Historical Branch, Ministry of Defence, Naval Staff Histories: Series editor, Captain Christopher Page, Frank Cass Publications, 2000.
2. Sir John Colville, *The Fringes of Power: Downing Street Diaries 1939–55*, Hodder & Stoughton, 1985.
3. Macleod, R. and Kelly, Denis (eds), *The Ironside Diaries*, Constable & Robinson, 1962.
4. Bond, Brian (ed.), *Chief of Staff: The Diaries of Lieutenant General Sir Henry Pownall*, vol. I, Leo Cooper, 1972.
5. Macleod and Kelly, *Ironside Diaries*.
6. Bond, *Chief of Staff*.
7. As a point of general interest, amongst those anti-tank units were batteries from the 65th Anti-Tank Regiment Royal Artillery TA, which was the Norfolk Yeomanry.
8. Jackson, *The Fall of France*, from page 88, by permission of Oxford University Press.
9. Ismay, Lord, *The Memoirs of Lord Ismay*, William Heinemann Ltd., 1960. Reprinted by permission of The Random House Group Ltd.
10. Bond, *Chief of Staff*.
11. Macleod and Kelly, *Ironside Diaries*.
12. Alanbrooke, *War Diaries*, diary entry for 23 May 1940.
13. Caddick-Adams, Peter, 'Anglo-French Co-operation during the Battle of France', from Professor Brian Bond and Michael Taylor (eds), *The Battle for France and Flanders Sixty Years On*, Leo Cooper, 2001.
14. Ellis, *The War in France and Flanders*.
15. Sebag-Montefiore, *Dunkirk*, Hastings.
16. *Ibid.*

CHAPTER 7

'Unable to face the bayonet at close quarters.'

SHORTLY BEFORE DAWN ON 18 May, the SS Totenkopf (Death's Head) Division had moved out of its base at Kassel, between Cologne and Bonn, in order to provide support for the rapidly advancing Panzers. With so many other German units on the move, the roads were initially heavily congested. Caught in lengthy traffic jams, the men of the Totenkopf, evidently considering themselves of such importance that they should be given priority, angrily threw insults and argued with other army commanders for right of way.

As a fighting formation, the Division was only seven months old, having come into existence during October 1939. In the early months of 1940, the Totenkopf was not considered to be as combat ready as some of the other Waffen-SS divisions, and was initially assigned a reserve role, in preparation to exploit and consolidate the Panzer breakthroughs. Though untested in battle, the men's loyalty and the military skills they appeared to have acquired in a short space of time, created a favourable impression on General von Weichs when he inspected them on the eve of the invasion.

The Totenkopf's roots ran deep into the evil ideals of Nazism, where political opposition, or the perceived threat of opposition, was not to be tolerated. During the purge of the SA (the Brownshirts) by the SS in the summer of 1934, when the Berlin garrison of the Leibstandarte began arrests, it was assisted by the SS Totenkopfverbände – guards from the concentration camp at Dachau, led by their brutal commandant, Theodor Eicke. He was responsible for killing Ernst Röhm, leader of the SA, at Stadelheim Prison in Munich on 1 July. Accompanied by two of his men, Eicke entered Röhm's cell and told him that he had forfeited his life. Obeying Hitler's instruction, Eicke placed before Röhm newspapers carrying reports of the 'Night of the Long Knives', together with a loaded pistol. After waiting outside the cell for over ten minutes, Eicke suspected that Röhm was not prepared to take the honourable way out, so he re-entered the cell and shot Röhm through the head.[1]

Eicke, who had been born in Alsace forty-eight years before and had served as an army paymaster during the First World War, was a former member of the SA. He was rewarded by Hitler with promotion to SS-Gruppenführer (Major General) and was appointed Führer of SS Guard Formations and Inspector of Concentration Camps.

While in charge at Dachau, he turned his guards into what he believed to be 'an outstanding body of men showing a splendid corps spirit'. They were expected to stand 'as matchless soldiers even in peacetime, day and night against the enemy, against the enemy behind the wire'. Rudolph Höss, commandant of Auschwitz, said that Eicke instilled into his camp guards 'a hate, an antipathy, against the prisoners which was inconceivable to those outside'. Furthermore, he despised the *Wehrmacht* and even viewed some of the other SS formations with contempt.

In October 1939, Dachau concentration camp was temporarily cleared of prisoners to allow for the formation of the Division as a fighting force. By this time the Totenkopfverbände was made up of five regiments: Oberbayern (based Dachau); Brandenburg (based Buchenwald); Thuringen (based Sachsenhausen);

Ostmark (based Mauthausen); and the newly formed Dietrich Eckhardt.[2]

Camp guard duties were taken over by elderly reservists and those men deemed unfit for front-line service, and also young Totenkopf recruits below the age of conscription. These became known as the Totenkopf Wachsturmbanne.

Seven months later, the Division advanced through Belgium and France where it had been assigned to General Hermann Hoth's XV Panzer Corps.

Elements of the Totenkopf gained their first experience of battle when they ran into one of the two British tank columns near Wailly, south-west of Arras, during the counter-attack on 21 May. The allegation that the Totenkopf fled from the field in large numbers is an exaggeration – it has to be remembered that they were inexperienced. Even Rommel's more experienced men were thrown into disarray by their inability to halt the British advance. As stated in the previous chapter, Rommel himself exaggerated the British strength, by reporting hundreds of tanks and five divisions. He appears to have taken great delight in also reporting that the SS Totenkopf had 'panicked'. One SS supply column had come under such a determined British attack that the troops did flee in confusion. SS gunners found that their 37mm anti-tank guns were ineffective against Matilda tanks – the shells just bounced off their thick frontal armour. One Matilda is said to have taken fifteen hits and came out of the battle with a few dents. As the British pressed on, the German anti-tank crews were forced to retreat and sought cover with the Totenkopf infantry in a nearby village. Arming themselves with grenades, they formed themselves into small tank-hunting parties but their efforts were successfully repulsed.

Just as Rommel rallied his men so Eicke did likewise with his SS. Heavier anti-tank fire supported by unopposed dive-bombing attacks and the lack of British reserves eventually stalled the counter-attack. Figures drawn from contemporary German sources gives the Totenkopf's casualties as nineteen killed, twenty-seven wounded and two missing. A more recent study by Tim Ripley gives slightly higher figures of thirty-nine dead, sixty-six wounded and two missing.[3]

The Totenkopf had been initiated into the stark reality of war. Unlike 'the enemy behind the wire', helpless and brutalized in concentration camps, the enemy now faced in the fields of France had a nasty tendency to shoot back with a ferocity that belied their diminishing numbers. Eicke, however, was desperate to prove his division's effectiveness as a fighting formation. He had instilled into his troops the need for fast-moving, highly aggressive attacks which required a mind set that treated death with contempt. But there were those within the ranks that treated life itself with contempt and were imbued with such arrogance that any opposition, no matter how courageous, required retribution.

Eicke's aggressive tactics were apparent from the moment his advanced units reached the Canal Line on 23 May. He immediately sent men across a sector of La Bassée Canal without carrying out a reconnaissance first. Finding themselves in an exposed position, the SS troops came under heavy British artillery and mortar fire.

Eicke then decided to bring up his own artillery in a somewhat belated attempt to support his stricken men.

Early the next day assault engineers completed a bridge over the canal and Eicke himself led the first wave of troops across. Again they became pinned down by shell- fire, but once a second wave had crossed a small bridgehead was established – not for long, however. Eicke was thwarted by his own side with the halt order from von Rundstedt's HQ. By the time the Totenkopf withdrew: forty-two had been killed, 121 wounded and five were missing.

Eicke was enraged but there was little he could do. Although he may have once been a king in his own sordid world of concentration camps, on the battlefield his formation was only one cog in the German war machine, subject to orders from superiors just like all the other units.

General Erich Höppner, the Corps Commander, harboured serious doubts about the reliability of the Totenkopf. Because of their high casualties, he went to their sector to assess the situation for himself. Eicke's stated indifference to the losses in manpower, and his assertion that in the face of the enemy the SS did not retreat, angered Höppner. Eicke was reprimanded 'in front of his own staff', Höppner accusing him of 'caring nothing for the lives of his own men, and even allegedly calling him a butcher'.[4]

Until the halt order was rescinded, the Totenkopf could only regroup and prepare for the major assault. However, 'British artillery and mortars were starting to take an increasing toll of the Totenkopf, so Eicke ordered a series of raids over the "Canal Line" by small SS squads to try and put the British guns out of action.'[5] Reconnaissance patrols were also sent across but failed to return, while engineers tried to mine the canal banks on the British side.

As the four companies of Norfolks moved to their positions by the Canal d'Aire during the early hours of Saturday, 25 May, 'C' Company, on the left, ran into Germans but succeeded in driving them back across the canal, suffering two casualties during the fighting.

Once 'A' and 'C' companies had confirmed that they were in position, Battalion HQ awaited news of 'B' and 'D', but as time passed nothing was heard from them. Patrols sent out from 'A' and 'C' companies failed to make contact.

At 0330 hrs, the men stood to. Initially the front was relatively quiet but with increasing daylight came the Luftwaffe. Its planes flew deep and largely unhindered over Allied territory for much of the day. German machine-guns opened fire in the area of 'C' Company's positions, but 'A' Company reported little activity in their sector at the time.

At around 0600, Battalion HQ heard from 'D' Company, who reported that they were in position and in touch with 'B'. Second Lieutenant Willeson, accompanied by runners, was sent forward to investigate and found that they were in the wrong place.

The total frontage to be defended by the depleted ranks of Holy Boys was around 2 miles, from the Bois de Pacqueat, just west of the road leading from the canal, to Le Cornet Malo, along the canal to north of Avelette. 'B' Company was supposed to be on the right of the battalion line, then 'A' and 'D' respectively forming the centre, with 'C' on the left flank. The canal runs in a south-easterly direction along much of that frontage then bends sharply southwards to Béthune. Just outside the town, the canal forks: one branch leads into Béthune; the other skirts the town to the north.

Under cover of darkness, lacking an accurate map and with fatigue weighing heavily on both bodies and minds, the companies had taken up positions, according to Captain Long, 'on branch canal in error'. They were facing Béthune and were too far forward. As a result, a gap existed between 'A' and 'C' companies, a gap that would have to be filled temporarily until 'B' and 'D' could move to their correct positions. Owing to lack of cover, the readjustment could not take place until dark and so the Battalion's Pioneer Platoon was ordered to fill the gap by taking up position on 'C' Company's right. There were only twenty Pioneers left, eight having already been lost by this time. According to Ernie Farrow:

What they told us to do was to go up on the top of this canal bank and make sure that every round that we fired got a German. We were getting short of ammunition and we must try and make every round count. I was using my .303 rifle. Occasionally we took turns in firing the Bren gun but there again we had to be very careful. We found that by using the rifles we could save quite a lot of ammunition. We could pick a German off with our rifle just as well as we could do with the Bren gun, where you'd fire probably twenty rounds to hit the same German. After we'd fired a certain amount of rounds, we'd got to scramble back down the bank of the canal, run along a bit, then go to the top again, just to try and bluff the Germans that there was a great company of us there. We were being hard pressed. We were being machine-gunned, mortared, shelled . . .

We were dug in our little foxholes and we'd keep our heads down but you couldn't be there all the time. You had to get up and fire at the Germans on the other side because those Germans were trying to get across the canal to get at us. The more we were hiding up, the less chance we had of stopping them.

Later that morning, the Pioneers received some support from a unit of machine-gunners. Commanded by Sergeant Kelly, the remains of 'B' and 'D' companies of the Manchester Regiment, numbering four machine-guns, reported to Battalion HQ. (Captain Long states that it was the 1st Battalion Manchester Regiment. It seems likely, however, on studying the listing of units which took part in the campaign that it was the 2nd Battalion, which is listed as Corps Troops under I Corps as Infantry – Machine-Gun.) Two gaps in the line could now be covered: the one already being filled by the Pioneers and another on the left flank.

'C' Company had been unable to locate any force on their left. The Lancashire Fusiliers were there because it later transpired that they had been sending out patrols in an attempt to make contact with the Norfolks. A French unit was supposedly in the gap but certainly not in position when sections from 'C' Company patrolled the area. This meant that there was a gap of around 1,200 yards exposing the Norfolk's left flank. Sergeant Kelly and his machine-gunners were ordered to take up a position near 'C' Company and cover the left flank. They were also told to support the Pioneers by giving fire across their front.

Captain Long wrote that the enemy:

attacked weakly during the morning at bridges A & B. Although bridges destroyed large numbers of barges were floating in canal – some were sunk. It was extremely difficult to do this – the enemy managed to push small parties of infantry over these barges – All attacks repulsed – enemy had not discovered our weakness in centre sector & made no attempt to cross canal there confining his efforts to the two bridges.

At midday, when Major Ryder set out for Brigade HQ, Acting Major Elwes took temporary command as Major Richardson was missing.

Fighting continued all along the front: 'D' Company engaged Germans who had presumably crossed the canal in their sector; 'C' Company came under frequent attacks which grew heavier as the hours passed; Battalion HQ came under fire and although all attacks were beaten off, they were taking their toll of the Battalion's overall strength.

In such a tense situation, any movement in the vicinity aroused suspicion. Fire was opened on some figures seen moving along a small road until it was established that they were French civilians and disorganized French soldiers. 'One old civilian,' wrote Long '& later one French soldier were detained for interrogation – When circumstances permitted French civilian released & French soldier joined Bn as a combatant.'

With the deathly cacophony of conventional warfare all around, Brigade HQ issued a warning of a more sinister threat: a silent killer, an impending gas attack. Pulling on their respirators, the men waited and hoped that their protection was adequate. How quickly the forward companies were warned was probably as fast as a man could run or some kind of vehicle could travel, assuming that they got through at all. Captain Long reveals that they were short of telephone cable at the time and, although Battalion HQ was connected to Brigade, there was insufficient cable to connect the four companies, especially as some of their positions were uncertain. Fortunately, the gas attack was a false alarm, but with such a lack of vital communication, there were periods when Battalion HQ had no idea what was happening in the company sectors. Had there been a link to 'A' Company at this time, then the worrying question of Major Ryder's prolonged absence would have been answered.

Brigade could only tell them that he had left l'Epinette at around 1430, but instead of returning to his own HQ, he had gone to 'A'

Company where he set about organizing a counter-attack against a German penetration of the Bois de Pacqueat. To bolster 'A' Company's strength, a company from the Lancashire Fusiliers was brought in. By this time, the Norfolks' Carrier Platoon under Second Lieutenant Elson had returned. The War Diary of 4th Infantry Brigade stated that on 23 May: 'At approx 1700 Carrier Pls of 4 In Bde under 2/Lt Edie, 1/Scots were taken to augment Polforce.' They had been deployed near Don on the Canal de la Deule which lies some 13 miles to the east of the Norfolks' positions on the Canal d'Aire.

Second Lieutenant Elson met Major Ryder at the crossroads outside Le Cornet Malo shortly after 1430, and the attack was planned and launched to drive the Germans from the wood. Led by Acting Captain Yallop, the men of 'A' Company, with the Lancashire Fusiliers under Second Lieutenant Spears, in support, moved into the Bois de Pacqueat, bayonets fixed. Through a storm of machine-gun and rifle fire, the Holy Boys rushed the enemy. Men fell wounded and dying, but those who made it through to face the Totenkopf at close quarters had the grim satisfaction of driving them out of the wood. In the words of Captain Long, the enemy was 'unable to face the bayonet at close quarters'.

With Major Ryder directing operations, Elson's carriers were split into two groups. Positioning themselves on either side of the road leading to the bridge, they advanced driving the Germans back towards the canal. At the bridge, however, German resistance stiffened considerably and they managed to hold on to a small house on the right of the road close to the canal. They could not be dislodged and the Norfolks were unable to recapture the bridge.

It was a costly action. Acting Captain Yallop was killed and 'A' Company lost about half its strength, mainly from light machine-gun fire before even getting to close quarters with the Germans. Two of the carriers were destroyed. 'We lost Mr Elson, Jackson and Heathfield,' said Lance Sergeant Alden of the Carrier Platoon, 'it was a wonder any of us returned.' Elson was posted as missing, believed killed but later reports stated that he had been wounded and taken prisoner. (It was while a prisoner of war that he helped Captain Long compile the report on the Battle of La Bassée.)

As dusk began to fall, Battalion HQ, still unaware of the CO's whereabouts, issued orders for the errant 'B' and 'D' companies to commence moving to their correct positions. Captain Hastings was sent out with a small party to reconnoitre the route to their new HQ at Le Paradis. The move was scheduled to begin at midnight.

Even though the firing had largely died down, there was little respite for the remaining Holy Boys. Parties of Germans remained active, probing defences and even attempting to repair one of the canal bridges. 'C' Company, who reported constant enemy activity in their area, sent out a patrol along a section of the canal. Company HQ also organized a patrol led by Lieutenant Woodwark to try and make contact with patrols from 'A' Company and to check for any Germans in a wood behind the HQ. The patrol returned at around 2330, reporting that the immediate area was clear of Germans but that they had not been able to make contact with 'A' Company.

Just before midnight, with the vehicles ready to transport personnel and equipment to Le Paradis, Major Ryder returned. They set off immediately. The journey along dark country roads, which threaded their way through rich, almost fen-like, farmland, latticed by dykes, took about half an hour. At 0030 on the morning of Sunday 26 May, the convoy reached the farm of Monsieur Henri Duriez. It was to be the Royal Norfolks' last Headquarters.

Notes

1. The account of Röhm's killing by Eicke is derived from Williamson, Gordon, *The SS: Hitler's Instrument of Terror*, Sidgwick & Jackson, 1994, and McGeoch, Angus, *The Third Reich at War*, Veranov, Michael (ed.), Magpie Books, an imprint of Constable and Robinson, 2004.
2. Williamson, *The SS*.
3. Ripley, Tim, *Hitler's Praetorians: The History of the Waffen-SS 1925–1945*, Spellmount, 2004. Reproduced by kind permission of The History Press.
4. Ailsby, Christopher, *Waffen SS: An Unpublished Record 1923–1945*, Sidgwick & Jackson, 1999).
5. Ripley, *Hitler's Praetorians*.

CHAPTER 8

'Operation Dynamo is to commence.'

W HILE THE HOLY BOYS had been staving off the German
incursions along the Canal d'Aire, Lord Gort was
finally forced to abandon British participation in
General Weygand's proposed counter-attack. Army Group B had
penetrated the Belgian sector on the River Lys near Courtrai,
seriously endangering the left flank of the BEF's II Corps. Lord
Gort wrote:

> The pattern of the enemy pincer attack was becoming clearer.
> One movement from the south-west on Dunkirk had already
> developed and was being held; the counterpart was now devel-
> oping on the Belgian front. The gap between the British left
> and Belgian right, which had been threatening the whole day,
> might at any time become impossible to close: were this to
> happen, my last hope of reaching the coast would be gone.

Gort reinforced II Corps flanks with what reserves he had available: the two divisions, the 5th and 50th which had been scheduled
to take part in Weygand's attack towards the south. Gort made his
decision unilaterally at 1800 on 25 May, without conferring with
the British War Cabinet or his French counterparts. Within
twenty-four hours, London, realizing that the Commander-in-
Chief's position was rapidly becoming untenable, approved his
decision. General Blanchard, too, who shared Gort's concern
about the Belgian line, called off his part in the counter-attack
during the evening of the 25th and ordered his troops to prepare
to move north, ready to help form a bridgehead at Dunkirk.
Weygand approved the order the next day.

116

So by 26 May, the disposition of the BEF was taking its final shape, as Gort explained:

Starting from what could be described as a normal situation with Allied troops on the right and left, there had developed an ever lengthening defensive right flank. This had become a semi-circular line, with both flanks resting on the sea, manned by British, French and Belgians. Later the position became a corridor in shape. The southern end of this corridor was blocked by the French First Army; and each side was manned, for the greater part of its length, by British troops. Next to the sea were the French troops on the west, and French and British troops on the eastern flank.

The immediate problem was to shorten this perimeter. British and French forces were together holding a front of 128 miles of which 97 miles were held by British troops, though some sectors were held jointly with the French. The virtual closing of Dunkirk as a port of entry was making a supply situation ever more difficult, and the ammunition situation permitted only of very restricted expenditure.

Of those 128 miles, the battered, dishevelled and exhausted remnants of 2nd Royal Norfolks were trying to defend a frontage of some 2 miles. Yet in the face of such a mission impossible, those few hundred men made a monumental effort to hold that corner of France. In so doing, they upheld and enhanced the reputation of the Regiment they served. In summarizing the character of the Royal Norfolk Regiment, Lieutenant General Sir Brian Horrocks said that:

[it] has always been renowned for its steadfastness and reliability in difficult situations. It is in fact the sort of Regiment which all commanders like to have available in order to plug a difficult gap. This staunchness had been developed over the years, for wherever the fighting was fiercest, climatic conditions most vile and the odds against victory most daunting, the 9th Foot was sure to be there.[1]

Under cover of darkness the two errant companies had moved into their correct positions and by first light on Sunday, 26 May had dug in. 'D' Company had moved into the gap between 'A' and 'C' companies and 'B' to the right of 'A' in the area of Le Cornet Malo.

The Pioneers, who had been filling the gap between the companies, were relieved during the night and set off for Battalion HQ only to find it had moved – they had no idea where. Ernie Farrow and a lance corporal scouted around in the darkness looking for other Holy Boys. Eventually they came across some men from 'A' Company who gave them the new position of Battalion Headquarters. As the Pioneer Platoon had been split into sections, Farrow and the NCO 'found some of the men had been wounded, and after giving what treatment they could, helped them back to HQ at Duries [sic] Farm, Le Paradis'.[2]

There, in the cowshed, Farrow saw other wounded – some who had lost a foot, others an arm – being tended by those bandsmen who were able to administer first aid. The first thing he wanted was a cigarette.

'I wanted a fag,' he said. 'I was dying! I'd never smoked a lot but this time [it was] to save my nerves.'

Eventually he found someone who had some and just smoked his head off for a few minutes.

At 0330, the Germans launched an attack against 'C' Company consisting of small parties armed mainly with sub machine-guns. But on the right a much heavier attack went in on 'A' and 'B' companies' positions near Le Cornet Malo. A damaged bridge leading to the village appeared to have been repaired sufficiently by German engineers to allow for the passage of tanks. Supported by an intense and very accurate mortar barrage along the whole front, which not only kept the other companies pinned down but also caused heavy casualties, the Germans advanced on Le Cornet Malo. Fighting in the village was fierce. 'A' Company of the Royal Scots came in to assist at the Bois de Pacqueat. Captain Long stated that the enemy were driven out by counter-attacks from 'A' and 'B' companies supported by the Scots.

It also appears that the remaining mortar supporting this area was running low on ammunition and Brigade was very slow in arranging for further supply.

A high price was being paid for resolute defence. Manpower at Le Cornet Malo soon reached a critical level and Duriez Farm received a message 'from "A" & "B" Coys stating that they had been badly smashed and were useless as a force'.

Captain Hasting was sent forward to asses the situation. At Le Cornet Malo he came across Second Lieutenant Slater, who had taken over command of 'A' Company following Captain Yallop's death the previous afternoon, standing helplessly at the crossroads with seven men. Their position by the canal had been overrun by Panzers, and, apart from a few wounded who were sheltering in a nearby house, the men with Slater were now the sum total of his company.[3]

While Hastings stood contemplating what action he should take, a senior officer arrived in the shape of Lieutenant Colonel Money, CO of the Royal Scots, anxious to hear Slater's story. Instead of trying to organize and advise the younger officers, Money took exception to a phrase Slater used when he said that his company had been 'minced up'. In what can only be described as a blimpish outburst, Money stormed on, for some time, about the casualties his own battalion had suffered and that he was 'far from being minced up'.[4] There was probably some inter-regimental rivalry colouring his attitude, especially in the light of the unfortunate incident at Bierges near Wavre, but considering the situation being faced, it was totally irresponsible for a senior officer to bluster like a caricature rather than take temporary control.

Left to his own devices, Hastings decided that Slater and his men should withdraw to Battalion HQ.

Hastings' departure was delayed by the arrival of Lieutenant Edgeworth who was commanding 'B' Company, although his total strength had been reduced to nineteen men. Their position was along the line of a hedge about 200 to 300 yards in front of the crossroads. Although there appeared to be no Panzers in the immediate vicinity at that moment, Edgeworth thought that there were Germans in the village just in front of his position.[5]

When Captain Hastings reported to Major Ryder at Duriez Farm, his decision to withdraw Slater and the remains of his company was not well received. As Hastings later wrote: 'he [Ryder] did not agree . . . and was angry that I had done it. "Go back," he said. "Put the two companies together and command them yourself." The crossroads, he told me, were to be held at all costs – to the last man and the last round. He concluded his orders by saying: "Keep them back with your pistol if necessary."[6]

Hastings saluted, left the farm building, climbed into his car and set off for Le Cornet Malo again. Meanwhile, the Battalion was 'reinforced' by the timely arrival of Sergeant Doughty and seven men who had just come back from leave. They were sent straight into the fray.

Captain Long, who was to follow Hastings and assist in organizing the position, took Ryder's car, an old Humber. Sections of the road were being raked by German machine-guns. Gathering a few men he found sheltering in ditches and houses, he led them to Le Cornet Malo.

By the time Long reached the position, Hastings' meager contingent had been bolstered by some fifty men of 'A' Company, Royal Scots who had been assisting in the area. Their Commanding Officer, Major Bucher, had been wounded and told his men to withdraw to their Battalion HQ.

Hastings, no doubt with Colonel Money's tirade still echoing through his mind, had stood squarely in the road, pistol in hand, and told the Scots to stop their withdrawal. He then explained to the NCO in charge, Sergeant Major Johnstone, 'that the cross roads had got to be held at all costs, and that there was to be no withdrawal by anybody beyond this point, and I should need his men to reinforce the position I was about to make. He made no demur. I think he was very pleased to have found an officer to tell him what to do.'[7]

The fifty Royal Scots, Edgeworth's nineteen, Slater's seven, and the few men brought by Captain Long, probably brought the number to around eighty.

> A line established along a hedgerow [that had previously been held by the remnants of 'B' Company under Lieutenant Edgeworth] & astride the road to the Wood – Heavy machine gun fire & mortar fire on area – Casualties small. Serious lack of spades and picks. Captain Hastings, Lts Willeson & Edgeworth [sadly Edgeworth was killed later that day] remained with Coys in order to fully arrange the final defended posts. Royal Scots took over area between road & wood.[8]

Major Bucher, the Scots' Company Commander, had managed to struggle back from their original position and despite his wounds insisted on staying with his men. Subsequently, when the need arose to issue orders, Sergeant Major Johnstone carried Bucher around on his back.[9]

Long drove back to Duriez Farm noting that 'Many wounded were being evacuated by 15 cwts [trucks] from forward positions.' He reported to Major Ryder that the position had been consolidated.

'Fire now died down in our area,' he wrote, 'but very heavy gun fire on left & heavy small arms from our near left.' By this time, all the Norfolks' companies could communicate with Battalion HQ by field telephone. 'Bn HQ connected with Bde – Main lines to B & C Coys with A & D Coys teed into main line.'

Major Richardson, missing since the previous afternoon, reached Duriez Farm shortly after Captain Long's arrival. He had been cut off while on patrol for 'D' Company and had spent the night with Germans between him and the company position. He said that the enemy appeared to be present in very large numbers.

Richardson's bleak assessment was corroborated by Brigadier Warren when he arrived at the Norfolks' HQ at 1100 hrs. He told them that 'the position was serious and that opposition was greater than had appeared at first. Orders "Last man, last round."'

The Royal Scots were now fully deployed on the Norfolks' right in order to try and consolidate the divisional line between 4 and 6 Brigades. Colonel Money's HQ had been moved from Calonne and set up in Le Paradis. 'A' Company had linked with the Holy Boys and was manning the defences organized by Hastings and Long in the Le Cornet Malo, Bois de Pacqueat area. 'B' Company was behind 'A' between the Bois de Pacqueat and Le Paradis. 'C' was on the far right of 4 Brigade's sector between the Bois de Pacqueat and the left flank of 6 Brigade's area. 'D' Company was in reserve at Le Paradis.

Looking at the broader picture across the whole of the 2nd Division's sector, the front was coming under extreme pressure. The arm of the iron claw that was the German pincer movement was still being held open but was certain to shut sooner or later. In summarizing the situation, the Official History noted that 4 Brigade was holding the Germans at the Bois de Pacqueat. This, as we have already seen, had been achieved by the Norfolks and a company from the Royal Scots.

On the divisional right, 6th Infantry Brigade had been forced to fight their way forward in an attempt to reoccupy the Canal Line because of a German bridgehead at Aire-sur-la-Lys. A mile short of their objective they were halted. The 1st Royal Welch Fusiliers, on the Brigade's left flank, was forced back, with heavy losses, on St Venant where the 2nd Battalion Durham Light Infantry were. One company of the Welch Fusiliers found themselves completely isolated in Robecq. Surrounded, they fought on until only a handful was left.

German Panzers had pushed through the line between Robecq and St Venant, and were bearing down on Merville which lies just over 2 miles to the north of Le Paradis. A Pioneer Battalion, the 6th King's Own Royal Regiment, supported by one field gun, held the German advance at a bridge south of Merville. They succeeded in knocking out three tanks, two armoured cars and took twenty prisoners before receiving meager reinforcements that night.

On the Division's left, 5 Brigade had prevented the Germans from advancing on Estaires. 'But here, behind Béthune,' says the Official History, 'he won a small bridgehead, and there were signs that he was massing for a more formidable breakthrough. It was in fact the opening of a battle in which the 2nd Division was to fight to the finish while the first moves in the general withdrawal took place behind them.'

After the Brigadier's departure, Major Ryder took the opportunity of reorganizing his officers. Major Richardson was appointed Second in Command, a post that had remained vacant since 21 May. Lieutenant Woodwark of 'C' Company was placed in command of 'A'. The Motor Transport Officer, Captain Hallett, was to command what was left of 'B' Company, and Second Lieutenant Buchanan was to lead 'D' Company. Second Lieutenant Jones of 'D' Company assumed command of the carriers while Second Lieutenant Merritt took over Hallett's role of MTO. Captain Hastings was to command HQ Company. Captain Long noted that they were 'able to put twelve officers in the line'.

Hastings' immediate task was to turn Battalion HQ into a strongpoint, capable of all-round defence. Standing beside the Rue du Paradis, which connected the village with Le Cornet Malo, Duriez Farm and its outbuildings stood on three sides of a court-yard in the centre of which was a pond. On the southern side was the farmhouse itself, three storeys high and with two cellars. The topmost window opened onto a commanding view of the country-side. On the western and northern sides were the farm's outbuildings including a substantial brick-built byre. The fourth side, the eastern side, completed the enclosure with a high brick wall pierced by a gate.

Loopholes were knocked into the brick walls or wrenched by crowbars into those buildings with corrugated-iron walls. Corrugated iron would certainly not stop bullets or shell fragments, so as extra protection for the rifleman, Hastings reinforced these firing positions with bales of straw.[10]

Under the circumstances, it was the best that could be done. The defenders of Duriez Farm knew that they would have to try to hold out against artillery fire, mortar rounds, grenades, tanks and machine-guns. The question was for how long?

Shortly after Ryder had reorganized his officers, Major Richardson made a round of the company positions by carrier. There was little respite from the Totenkopf attacks but the defence put up by the decreasing number of Holy Boys was fierce. Encouragingly, German Panzers were being kept at bay with anti-tank rifles, LMGs. (light machine-guns) and grenades, and with the occasional support, on the left flank, from an Anti-Tank Regiment and a Brigade Anti-Tank Company.

At Le Cornet Malo, Captain Hallett took the fight to the Germans by leading a patrol from 'B' Company to the southern part of the village. With rifle and Bren-gun fire, they halted the SS men's advance from the canal. 'It was a pity,' Hallett recalled, 'we had no mortars or we could have bombed them beautifully.' However, his small party's firepower had been effective enough. When they moved forward, no opposition was encountered and the few surviving Germans gave themselves up. Hallett questioned one wounded German and found him quite willing to talk. 'He said,' wrote Hallett, 'that there was about a division against us across the canal, as I'd expected, instead of the odd hundred or so I'd been told.'[11]

As the fighting wore on across the whole front, the LMGs. were deteriorating through lack of spare barrels. Mortar ammunition began to run low and only after repeated demands were thirty rounds supplied.

'Very little artillery support,' wrote Captain Long, 'Field guns (except 2 in rear of D Coy) appeared to be absent.'

Reinforcements in the shape of a platoon of machine-gunners from the Argyll and Sutherland Highlanders arrived and were ordered to take up position behind 'A' and 'D' companies. Their task was to cover the canal from 'D' Company's front in an arc to the Bois de Pacqueat. Just to the right of the wood, the Norfolks deployed the carriers to reinforce the area between the wood itself and 'C' Company of the Royal Scots.

There was no support for the beleaguered ground forces from the air. The Luftwaffe had free rein for their observation aircraft to fly above the lines unchallenged and feed back information about the British dispositions. Some time during the day leaflets were dropped onto the Brigade area bearing a message from the *Wehrmacht*. The text, complete with misspellings, was reproduced in 4th Infantry Brigade's War Diary and reads as follows:

BRITISH SOLDIERS

Germans around! You are encircled! German
troupes invaded Courtrai, Tournai, Valenciennes,
Lillers, Aire, St Omer are occupied.
Calais will be taken immediately. Why do you fight further?
    Do you really believe this nonsens, that
Germans kill their prisoners? Come and see
yourselves the contrary!
    The match is finished! a fair enemy will be
fairly treated.

We know from leaflet drops in other sectors to what use the recipients put these appropriately sized pieces of paper.

Towards the end of the day, an uneasy calm settled over the battle-ravaged landscape. The line had held, but in parts was buckled and the resulting cost in manpower was high. Captain Long estimated that the Battalion numbered approximately 250 officers and men. In other words, the Holy Boys' strength had been reduced to just over two fully manned companies.

At 1857 hrs, the Admiralty had issued an historic signal: 'Operation Dynamo is to commence.' What could be salvaged of the BEF was to be evacuated from the Continent, but others would have to stay behind. Major Ryder told his men that they 'must be prepared for a heavy attack on the 27th'.

Ahead lay another day's fighting in which a handful of Davids had to try and hold back the Goliath of the Nazi War Machine. 'Every hour was now of importance,' said the Regimental History, 'and the battalion's part in stemming the German advance was helping to save countless lives.'

During the lull, as darkness gradually began to cloak the countryside, hot food was prepared and brought to Duriez Farm. Sergeant Gilding, formerly of the Mortar Platoon but at that time acting as Company Quartermaster Sergeant, recalled:

I arrived at the battalion headquarters at the farm somewhere between nine and ten that evening. There was very little to be seen. Major Ryder came forward and spoke to us and said that he was glad to see us and that the food could be distributed when he could get the people off the perimeter where they were out on various defensive positions. From then on we were feeding the lads as they were coming in in dribs and drabs. We had the signallers actually in the farmhouse itself and the riflemen were out in the buildings – the cowshed, the pigsties, even out in the little meadows around the farm – wherever they had taken up position.

We had special containers with lids that bolted down and kept it hot. There was no sound of shots, bombs, shellfire or anything. It went on like that all through the night till three o'clock in the morning. I was still there with the cook's wagon still dishing out for the odd people that had been pulled in. Major Ryder came in and said, 'The situation seems to be getting worse.' By this time it was just beginning to get daylight. 'I think you'd better pack up and get back to B Echelon. But before you go report to the farmhouse where we've got the Company Headquarters and take some of the documents away – they're not much use to us here!' By the documents he meant the equipment rolls and various paperwork. It was then that I started to hear what sounded like heavy vehicles, possibly tanks moving in the distance. Also the first mortar bomb landed in the battalion area.

Notes

1.   Horrocks, Lieutenant General Sir Brian, 'Royal Norfolk Regiment, A Special Introduction', in Carew, *The Royal Norfolk Regiment*, reproduced by courtesy of the Trustees of the Royal Norfolk Regimental Museum, Norwich.
2.   Jolly, *The Man who Missed the Massacre*.
3.   Sebag-Montefiore, *Dunkirk*, Hastings.
4.   *Ibid.*
5.   *Ibid.*
6.   *Ibid.*
7.   *Ibid.*
8.   Long, 'War Diary'.
9.   Sebag-Montefiore, *Dunkirk*, Hastings.
10.   *Ibid.*
11.   Sebag-Montefiore, *Dunkirk*, Hallett.

CHAPTER 9

'Little or no hope of an organized withdrawal in daylight.'

WHEN SERGEANT GILDING left Duriez Farm at 0330 on the morning of Monday, 27 May, heavy German vehicles, probably Panzers, could be heard moving in the distance. As mortar bombs landed, half a dozen or so hit the road in front of the truck giving the occupants 'quite a bumpy ride'.

'Put your foot down and get the hell out of this!' Gilding urged the driver.

B Echelon was about 1½ miles north of Le Paradis at l'Epinette. When they reached the area, Gilding found that 'everybody was packing up ready to move. The Quartermaster [Lieutenant Grant] had received a message from them saying that "The battalion were going to be staying in that position and that we were not to wait, that we were to go back to some other rendezvous."'

At the canal, the SS Totenkopf were preparing to smash their way through the stubborn resistance in order to reach their objective for the day, Bailleul, which lies roughly halfway between Le Paradis and the Belgian town of Ypres. Five miles north-east of Bailleul, over the Belgian border, lies Kemmel, the point at which the German pincer movement was to close. From the eastern sector, the Sixth Army of Army Group B had to fight its way through positions held by the BEF's 5th Division between Ypres and Comines – their target, Kemmel. The Kleist Group in the Fourth Army of Army Group A was to fight its way to Kemmel and Poperinge. Orders issued by German High Command stated that the objectives had to be reached on the 27th.

Within the loop of the Canal d'Aire, two fresh and as yet untried German SS motorized infantry units had taken up position between Hinges and Mont Bernanchon. Totenkopf Infantry Regiment 2 was commanded by Colonel Bertling and Totenkopf Infantry Regiment 3 was led by Lieutenant Colonel Goetz. Supported by the 4th Panzer Division and an SS artillery regiment they were to throw their full weight against the thin and exhausted khaki line in order to conform, at all costs, to their deadline and objective. The SS believed that they were up against élite British regiments and referred to the Holy Boys as the Norfolk Grenadiers.

Some hours before, as darkness had fallen, Captain Hallett's forward posts at Le Cornet Malo had come under attack and been driven back. He then became aware that the Germans were 'digging hard just beyond the village'. This went on all night but shortly before midnight he heard 'the unmistakable sound of tanks'. He sent out patrols to locate the German positions and then called in mortar fire. 'From the shouts and shrieks, there must have been some direct hits.'[1]

Just south of the nearby village of Riez du Vinage, the 1st Battalion of Totenkopf 2 had crossed the canal during the night by way of a repaired bridge: Pont Supplie. It was to be the Regiment's first experience of battle and proved to be a baptism of fire when immediate opposition was encountered from the defenders. August Leitl, a platoon commander in No. 3 Company of Totenkopf 2 said that they advanced through the darkness sheltering in ditches from British machine-gun fire. Defence of the houses held them up for long periods.[2]

Riez du Vinage was eventually taken and Totenkopf 2 harboured for a while in the Bois de Pacqueat. At dawn an assault was launched on Le Cornet Malo. No. 3 Company commanded by Captain Fritz Knoechlein was in the centre; No. 2 Company under Captain Stoeter on the right with Captain Kaltofen's No. 1 Company on the left in semi-reserve.

Knoechlein spoke of the slow progress they made as his platoons had to fight their way yard by yard through the straggling village. Losses were very heavy; a platoon commander was killed and No. 2 Platoon suffered particularly badly.

His battered company was given a brief respite from the fighting by the arrival of other Totenkopf troops. Dead comrades were collected and Knoechlein conducted a short burial service. He said that they had not died in vain but would continue to march along the road to victory. During the funeral oration, it was subsequently alleged, he had also spoken of 'revenging their deaths'.

Increasing numbers of Panzers were crossing the canal. 'Bridges now repaired & enemy able to cross at will,' observed Captain Long. 'Barges made further crossing possible.'

As well as using barges, Ernie Farrow recalled the Germans 'driving their lorries into the canal and trying to drive their tanks across these lorries'.

At around 0500 hrs, tanks appeared in 'B' Company's area: 'huge fellows,' wrote Hallett, 'and about a dozen. I phoned Battalion HQ . . . Then they cut the line. That was the last message I got to the battalion.'[3]

In the Signals Office, which had been set up in one of the cellars beneath the house at Duriez Farm, was Signaller Bob Brown. He later spoke of the moment when contact was lost. 'The tanks broke through and they ['B' Company] were the first to go out of communication. I was on the switchboard at the time and they were the first ones for us to lose.'

Only moments before, Brown had been talking to his friend, Alf Blake, 'B' Company's signalman.

'I'm afraid we're in for it,' Blake told him. 'Don't forget me. We had some good times together. I don't know whether I'll ever see you again.'[4]

It was the last Bob Brown ever heard of his friend.

Despite Captain Hallett's forward section falling back and leaving guns and anti-tank rifles behind, the remnants of 'B' Company defiantly faced the Panzers.

'Eventually,' wrote Hallett, 'we had a brainwave, and ran out below the tanks' angle of fire, and put Mills grenades in the tracks. It did not do the tanks much harm, but frightened the drivers, and they ditched them. We got four that way . . . Then gradually some form of order was restored. We got the LMG back in position, and the A/T rifles mounted.'

Initially, the Totenkopf infantry were way behind the Panzers, but when they arrived, they were, according to Hallett's description:

in masses. I never believed I'd see troops advancing shoulder to shoulder across the open, but these men did and they suffered accordingly. The Brens fired until they were red-hot, and also the riflemen . . . we also suffered heavily, and in the end, I was left in a big farm with an attic, with an A/T rifle, and a rifle for myself, and one rifleman to help.[5]

The rifleman was killed and Hallett was wounded but taken prisoner as he tried to escape.

Endeavouring to support the defenders of Le Cornet Malo was the sole remaining mortar team. Private Arthur Brough spoke of their desperate efforts to stem the advancing German tide:[6]

Lots of tanks and heavy gunfire; we were putting as much stuff down the mortar as we could to get rid of our ammunition. We were trying to repulse them but we knew it wasn't a lot of good because there were so many there . . . The mortar must have been red-hot. Anything they could get hold of they were putting down the mortar. There were only about three of us left by that time and Platoon Sergeant Major Ireland. He got shot. We resorted to rifle fire which was absolutely stupid but I suppose it was instinct to try and do your job. Then we saw it was absolutely hopeless. We chucked the bolts out of the rifle. Why you do these things don't ask me why, but I think it must be instinct. That's what you've been taught to do, immobilize your rifle, take the bolt out. Then we scattered. Tanks by the hundred were coming up. We just ran for it. What else can you do when you see tanks coming at you?

Brough, along with Johnny Cockerel, suffered leg wounds when hit by fragments from an exploding shell. For them, stopped in their tracks and sitting in a ditch, the battle was over and they were taken prisoner.

At about the same time that Hallett's company had first encountered the Panzers, Battalion HQ received some heartening news. Brigade informed them that a heavy counter-attack was expected from a French infantry brigade supported by a British tank regiment. It was to commence at 1000 hrs and in the meantime they were likely to see French officers in the sector carrying out a reconnaissance. The news was relayed to all companies, but by this time there was no link to 'B' Company. Had the counter-attack materialized at the appointed hour, it would have been much too late for the valiant defenders of Le Cornet Malo. According to Corporal Walter Fripes of the 2nd Platoon, No. 3 Company, Totenkopf 3, the village 'was occupied about 10 am on 27th May and prisoners taken were sent to the rear'.

Two hours before the capture of Le Cornet Malo, ten men from the Pioneer Platoon had returned to Duriez Farm, having spent the night in a ruined cottage supporting 'D' Company. Private Ernie Farrow said it was about 0800 and they were actually hoping to get some food. Almost immediately he found himself part of a small team of 'volunteers' detailed to destroy a bridge, the Pont d'Avelette.

'This bridge,' he explained, 'had been left intact to let our men over and artillery had been shelling all round it to stop the Germans getting across . . . the time was right for us to blow it.'

Lance Corporal 'Misler' Mason was to lead the party and selected his three volunteers by the usual army method: 'You, you and you!' – namely Farrow, Porter and Reeve.

There was too much equipment for the men to carry so Major Ryder allowed them to use his car and briefed his driver, Doug Auker, who came from King's Lynn. No map reference was needed as the bridge was only a short distance, around 3 miles away and Auker knew exactly where to go.

The boot of the old Humber was filled with amatol, gun cotton and primers, and just before they left they were handed some ammunition.

'Three rounds of ammunition,' said Farrow, 'to fight the German Army!'

A sergeant major presented them with a large tin of Bluebird toffees perhaps as recompense of sorts for being unable to obtain any food, although they were promised a hot meal on their return.

As they bumped along the road, the car came under sporadic shell and machine-gun fire.

'We knew,' said Farrow, 'that one bullet through the back of our car and we could all be blown to pieces. We hoped to God that the driver would get us there as quick as he could.'

Throughout the brief drive, they struggled to get the lid off the toffee tin, but had not succeeded by the time Auker called out that the bridge was in front. On their right was the canal and on their

left a large farmhouse, from which a German machine-gun immediately opened fire, riddling the car with bullets. Miraculously,
neither the occupants nor the explosives in the boot were hit by the
burst. Mason, Farrow, Porter and Reeve leapt out of the Humber
and headed into the canal.

> The driver was trying to turn his vehicle, to get back to head-
> quarters to warn them that the bridge had already been taken;
> I suppose that's what was in his mind. By the time we got into
> the canal we heard this hell of an explosion, and we were
> spattered by all the pieces of metal and whatnot as the poor
> old car was blown up and the driver with it.

Despite the odds, the four men decided to have a final crack at the
Germans. They scrambled as best they could up the steep slippery
bank and loosed off some rounds at the house, hoping that every
precious bullet would count. But they could not safely get out of
the canal at this point. With Germans on both sides they would
simply be picked off.

'Right,' said Mason, 'bolts out of your rifles, get rid of them,
because there's no way they're needed any more.'

All surplus equipment, including their tin hats, was discarded
and they swam away hoping to find a safer spot.

Eventually Mason stopped them and told them to stay where
they were and to keep their heads down. 'I'm going to swim down
the canal and find somewhere where there's a ditch runs into the
canal where we can climb out. That's the only way we can get out.
We can't get out where we are now.'

With those words the Lance Corporal swam away. The three
remained close together in the rushes: Farrow in the middle, Porter
on his left and Reeve on the right. Porter came from Beccles and
had joined the Army at the same time as Farrow early in 1938.
Instead of keeping his head down, however, Porter decided to have
a peep over the top. Farrow recalled:

> At that instant, I heard this machine-gun or rifle fire . . . I
> turned and looked up. The poor fellow had been shot right
> through the middle of his head and the back of his head was
> missing; as quick as that, and he was sinking back into the

water. I was trying to hold him up which was no good because he was already dead.

A few moments later, while talking to Reeve, who came from Dickleburgh and had served the Regiment for several years, Farrow felt something hit him in the face. He immediately placed his hand on the area where he had felt the impact and found that it was covered in blood.

'I looked at the blood and thought I'd been hit. I felt again but I was still all there.'

It was actually Reeve's jaw which had hit Farrow, ripped off by a shot. Farrow continued:

> He was then disappearing underneath. The last thing I saw of him was these two gold teeth shining in the top of his head, and for many, many weeks afterwards, whenever I opened my eyes, I could see his face with no chin and his gold teeth showing. The water round me was red with his blood. But the poor boys, they'd gone, they were at the bottom.

Mason returned a few minutes later. He had found a ditch abutting the canal from where they would be able to clamber out and hopefully make their escape. They slipped under the water and swam, coming up for air from time to time.

'Here we are,' said Mason presently.' You stop where you are; that's an order. Keep your head down. I'll go and see if there is anything on this meadow.'

While waiting, Farrow was sure that he saw a bush move on the left-hand side.

Then he heard a mouthful of army language.

> I looked and 'Misler' had been shot through the shoulder, and the bone of his arm was sticking out of the top. But they couldn't kill 'Misler' like that. He put his arm round my neck to keep himself up . . . This bush I'd seen, there was a German behind it, probably the one who had shot 'Mis'.
>
> Just then he came from behind this bush, jumped in this ditch and came running towards us. When he was about twelve yards from us, he stopped and put his rifle up to his

shoulder. I said my last prayer because I knew I was going to die. But the Lord was with me and there was a loud click. He'd run out of ammunition or his breech had stuck . . . He turned his rifle round, got hold of the barrel, and as he got close to us, he took a swipe at my head. I put my arm up to stop him hitting me, and the first blow smashed all my hand up. The next blow came down and I still had the strength to hold my elbow up and he just smashed my elbow and put my shoulder out of joint.

One more blow and I'd have been dead, but at that very instant, I heard a loud shout and lots more Germans came into sight. One of these was an officer who'd shouted. They jumped into the ditch and he ordered them to pull us out of the canal. They pulled out poor old 'Mis' first. They'd got to be very careful because if they pulled his wrong arm they'd have pulled it off, he was in such a bad state. But he was still alive and they put him on a stretcher and took him away. They pulled me out.

Back at Le Cornet Malo, Second Lieutenant Emile Stuerzbecher, Adjutant of 1st Battalion Totenkopf 2, had been ordered by his Battalion Commander, Major Fortenbacher, to set up HQ in the village. Stuerzbecher explained:

I proceeded with the headquarters section in the direction of the village. It was then midday. The assistant M.O. and some stretcher-bearers joined me. After about six hundred metres, we reached the edge of the village. The village was burning in several places, and the noise of battle was deafening. As we were standing on the edge of the village and I was trying to discover from returning wounded, ammunition carriers and so forth, what was going on in front, a man came and reported that wounded British were lying at the burning farm on the left. The assistant M.O. thereupon went with this man in the direction he indicated. After a few moments he called to me and I followed him. He was standing by a group of about twenty-five British solders lying and sitting on the ground, and was trying to converse with one of them, a doctor or some thing of the kind. I helped them with this and we found that medical supplies and water were needed urgently by the wounded men. The assistant M.O. ordered the removal of the wounded away from the burning stable to a nearby group of trees, which was subsequently done, with everybody helping. The M.O. said he would stay there awhile and see to the care of the wounded and I was able to return to the road. Hauptsturmführer [Captain] Knoechlein came running from the road shouting loud and very excited. He roared at the M.O. and myself, 'These prisoners are nothing to do with you. They belong to me.' My first impression of Knoechlein was that he had gone mad and only after some argument during which he insisted that the prisoners were his did he quieten down.

Stuerzbecher thought that Knoechlein may have wanted to add these prisoners to his list of captives for his own credit, but the Medical Officer would not allow them out of his care. Shortly afterwards a runner reached Stuerzbecher with orders from Fortenbacher, who was well forward, for heavy weapons and artillery to be brought up to break the British defence.

German testimony refers time and again to the strength of the British resistance, which continued for much of the day despite diminishing numbers. The British Official History quotes:

the following conclusion . . . recorded by XXXIX Corps in Hoth Group: 'As foreseen, the enforced two-day halt on the southern bank of the canal produced two results on 27th May:

1. The troops suffered considerable casualties when attacking across La Bassée Canal, now stubbornly defended by the enemy.
2. There was no longer time to intercept effectively the stream of French and English troops escaping westwards from the Lille area towards the Channel.'

Inexorably, the defenders were being worn down. 'Very heavy attacks at all points along the front,' wrote Captain Long. On 'C' Company's left, in the Lancashire Fusiliers' sector, motorized German units were seen moving along a road. Long continued:

Artillery support called for, not given. A & D reported heavy
attacks by tanks and infantry – Enemy tanks put out of action
in A Coy area by A/T rifle and Bren fire – No air support –
Enemy recce machines very active out of range of LMG –
Casualties extremely heavy but morale very high – Lt Willeson
wounded in arm and out of action – Enemy troops, infantry
and light artillery in action on right front of Bn HQ near Bois
de Pacqueat enemy mortar fire from there also.

As the Totenkopf continued to press forward, a company of
Royal Scots was seen to be falling back rather rapidly. If this was
allowed to continue, the Norfolks' right flank would be exposed.
Captain Gordon was sent to find out what was going on, stopped
the withdrawal and stayed with the contingent of Scots for the
remainder of the action.

Duriez Farm now came under fire from two Panzers which had
moved up on the left and halted beneath some trees about 400
yards away. The Holy Boys returned fire with a hail of machine-
gun and anti-tank rounds ensuring that the tanks did not come any
closer for the time being.

With artillery support so desperately needed, the arrival at the
Norfolks' HQ of crews who had been manning a section of field
guns, was not well received. They said their withdrawal had been
ordered by an 'Artillery officer'. Although out of touch with their
Battery Commander, they still had a good supply of ammunition.
Major Ryder told them to go back to their guns and follow all
orders issued by his HQ.

Contact with 'A' Company ceased. They were out of touch both
by wire and runner so it had to be assumed that their position had
been overrun. 'C' and 'D' companies, however, were still phoning
in and reported considerable German movement along the roads
on the left flank towards Locon. Again artillery support was
requested but none could be given.

'Last man, last round' – Major Ryder would endeavour to carry
out Brigadier Warren's order to the letter unless told otherwise. He
expected it of his own men and naturally enough of any other units
in his area. So when the Platoon of machine-gunners from the
Argyll and Sutherland Highlanders withdrew to Duriez Farm
complete with vehicles, plenty of ammunition, undamaged

weapons and light casualties, he would accept no excuse. The Lieutenant in charge, who Long does not name in his report, said that the enemy were too close and he no longer had infantry support. Ryder gave him a direct order to return to his former position and not to move unless ordered by the Norfolks' HQ.

'Platoon returned to position,' observed Long, 'but a few minutes later were seen leaving the area again leaving guns behind. The guns were served by men of 2/N until position rendered untenable.'

Soon after this incident, the crews of the field guns came back to the farm, having been ordered to withdraw by the mysterious 'Artillery officer'. Ryder felt that their position was probably impossible. With increasing numbers of Panzers and German infantry in the area there was little sense in sending out any of his men to investigate. He told them to throw the breech blocks of their guns into the pond in the courtyard, issued them with rifles and told them to join in the defence of the farm.

The fate of 'A' Company was confirmed when Lieutenant Woodwark and six men, the only survivors, reached Battalion HQ. Their position had indeed been overrun. Major Ryder approved Woodwark's action in getting the handful of men back and added them to the defenders of Duriez Farm.

Among the survivors of 'A' Company was Private Albert Pooley. He and three other men were detailed to take up position on one side of the courtyard where, with mortar bombs falling around them, they decided to protect their backs by piling up bales of straw. At one stage, mortar rounds started a fire in the farmhouse which was quickly extinguished.

Through a loophole in the wall, Pooley could look out across the landscape, over fields and meadows, to some houses along the Rue du Paradis. He noticed enemy soldiers moving behind the farm. Movement within the perimeter of the farm was becoming difficult and dangerous. He 'saw one man set up a range-finder in a doorway. He thought he was screened by the building, but just as he was bending over his instrument he was struck by a bullet in the shoulder . . . He seemed not only surprised but indignant, as though the Germans had done something they should not have done.'[7]

Suddenly there was a hiatus in the German attack. 'The enemy on our right,' wrote Long, 'were now seen to be getting up and running about confusedly – they appeared to be without a commander – Heavy fire was opened up on them and they retired to the Bois leaving an infantry gun behind.'

It was first assumed that the French and British counter-attack, about which they had been informed earlier in the day, had started elsewhere on the front, forcing the Germans into a temporary retirement in order to regroup. But there was no relieving attack. Ferocious defence had brought the inexperienced Totenkopf infantry regiments to a standstill.

In the open countryside around Le Paradis, the Germans suffered severely. One battalion lost all its company commanders so that NCOs had had to take charge of the battered companies. August Leitl spoke of how the defence of various houses held them up for long periods. 'We were very exposed,' he said. 'If somebody just lifted his head he was killed. The British used snipers very skilfully.'

Tim Ripley in *Hitler's Praetorians* summarized the Totenkopf's desperate situation:

> As the morning passed, however, the British defence stiffened and soon the SS attack had broken down into a series of vicious, small actions. As the casualties began to mount, Eicke started to struggle to regain control of his troops. By early afternoon the attack had ground to a halt. The divisional command post was in a chaotic state as Eicke tried to come up with a way to get the attack moving again. Amid the crisis, the divisional operations officer collapsed in the HQ from a haemorrhaging stomach ulcer.[8]

The taking of Le Paradis that day was essential if conformity was to be maintained with the lines of those divisions operating on the right and left. The Totenkopf had originally thought that their 3rd Regiment would encounter the stiffest opposition but this unit had made the better progress. If the British continued to prolong the defence of Le Paradis, then Totenkopf 3's left flank would be vulnerable.

An SS Major (whose identity was not revealed at the time of his interrogation at Bologna, Italy in 1948) was Totenkopf 2's ordnance officer. He was also responsible for maintaining the Regiment's War Diary and compiling daily reports of operations; he monitored incoming and outgoing orders. Radio reports from the front-line units spoke of 'savage fighting'. Artillery was taken forward and guns fired over open sights at close range.

Eventually, Eicke ordered this officer to go forward with instructions that the taking of Le Paradis was essential; all available reserves were to be used to protect Totenkopf 3's left flank.

Later, he was sent forward again by his Regimental Commander, Colonel Bertling, to ascertain from the battalion commanders the situation at Le Paradis. His journey by motorcycle took him to the heart of the fighting. He said that he found the commander of the 1st Battalion of Totenkopf 2 lying in a ditch at the crossroads just south of the church. The whole centre of Le Paradis around the church was strongly held and snipers were operating from the steeple. A house on the eastern boundary 'was being defended like a fortress'. He was unable to reach the commander of the 2nd Battalion without making a wide detour as the southern edge of the village was being savagely defended.

The officer said that the 1st Battalion had almost been wiped out, so orders were issued for the 3rd Battalion of Totenkopf 2, together with elements of Totenkopf 3, to complete the assault on Le Paradis.

The Regimental Commander of Totenkopf 3, Lieutenant Colonel Colonel Hans Friedmann Goetz, came with his men to execute the orders. On reaching the crossroads near Le Paradis church, he was killed by a sniper's bullet.

Duriez Farm was certainly being defended like a fortress. As we have already seen, details and stragglers from other units had joined the defenders. Captain Long noted an APTS Sergeant, a Cameron Highlander, a number of gunners and several from the Manchesters.

Signaller Bob Brown found himself keeping watch in a forward position beside a lance corporal from the Regimental Police. Major Ryder had ordered all surplus personnel out to the defence of Battalion HQ. Brown had handed his switchboard over to the wireless operator:

> I went out and the Adjutant, Captain Long, told me to go forward to a row of trees . . . and if I saw any Germans coming between the companies and us to let him know.
> I was there for some time and no sign of anybody, so I

withdrew about a hundred yards or so to a farm building. And there was a Lance Corporal in the Regimental Police in one of the buildings and between the two of us we kept watch, until he happened to look back towards Battalion Headquarters along the road. There was a German motor-cycle combination with a machine-gun mounted on it coming from behind us, from behind Battalion Headquarters. So between the two of us we stopped them, we fired and stopped the combination coming through. And then we had to get back to Battalion Headquarters and let them know they were round behind us. So the two of us dashed across the road as quickly as possible, crawled along the ditch to the farm and gave the information that we had.

I then took up position in the barn. We knocked holes through the galvanized walls which by this time were heavily riddled with shrapnel – there was holes and whatnot through them . . . mortar bombs were dropping over the barn and dropping behind us in between the farm buildings. A friend of mine I was with, John Hagan, said, 'We'll find somewhere a bit more safe.' We went to the end of the barn and there was a small brick building, outhouse. We went in there and knocked out bricks for loopholes and that's where we continued our defence for the remainder of the day, through this brick building which was more safe than the old galvanized barn was.

The other side of the farm was all the stables, cowsheds and barn stables. And the men there had done the same, they'd knocked bricks out and made loopholes. The opposite side of the farm buildings was a brick wall and the men that were available did the same there, so we were more or less all round defence. And that's what happened up till the end, we were being attacked from all sides.

An attack from the rear was now attempted by a German motor-cycle unit. Heavy fire drove them into a farm building just across the road where they set up a defensive position. They were too close for comfort and unleashed a fusillade on Battalion HQ. According to Captain Long it seemed impossible to get at them until Regimental Sergeant Major Cockaday took prompt and very courageous action. Grabbing a Bren gun, he charged into the open firing at the German position. Despite being hit, he remained in the open and kept the enemy occupied while Major Ryder, Company Sergeant Major Whitlam and a small party worked their way to the flank and attacked. The Germans were forced to fall back under fire until they reached the main body of their troops in the rear. Major Ryder halted his party at a hedgerow from where they fired again. Then, leaving Captain Long to organize the defence of this advanced post, Ryder returned to his HQ to inform Brigade of the development. The advanced post was subsequently reinforced.

Regardless of their heavy casualties, the Totenkopf tried to press home their attack. Mortar rounds and artillery shells rocked the farm buildings. At one stage British artillery rounds landed around Duriez Farm. The error was rectified immediately by Captain Long who, dodging through a hail of German bullets, made it to the Signals Office in the cellar and requested Brigade to stop their support.

> Enemy in strong force in rear & it was rapidly becoming evident that the Bn was becoming isolated. C Coy still reported enemy troop carriers & tanks moving around left flank. No artillery support in that area. Troop carriers moving round right flank in Le Paradis were engaged by artillery and suffered heavy casualties – Forward party retired to next house – this held till end – Enemy infantry working up ditches – Heavy fire from flanks and rear – Defended posts were now houses on right & left of road (rear of Bn HQ) Bn HQ farm house, yard and ditches surrounding, houses left and right of road & road block (front of Bn HQ) – all houses strongly fortified – Pte Edwards with LMG did excellent work all through this part of action.

Captain Long himself had done excellent work throughout. His conduct was exemplary and drew a warm tribute from Captain Hastings:

> Charles Long is a great success with the men. He is telling awful lies, but he talks as if he himself believes what he says . . . The men love him . . . He set a fine example by his disregard

of personal danger, and certainly did more than any other officer to keep morale at a high level. He has a breezy manner, was always cheerful, and full of unbounded optimism . . . All this he managed to convey to the troops.[9]

Grim news came through from 'D' Company: only Second Lieutenant Buchanan and five men were left. They had been driven back to their Company HQ where they would stand and fight. This was the last that Duriez Farm heard of them.

Soon after, as German fire intensified further on Battalion HQ, 'C' Company made contact. Acting Major Elwes informed them that his position was surrounded. He again requested artillery support but again there was none available in the area. The line fell silent. The signaller pressed the button of his field telephone set but to no avail. 'All Coys now cut off from Bn HQ' wrote Long.

Under the heading 'Last Phase of Battle', Captain Long summarized the situation as it was, according to his timing, at 1600 hrs. It makes poignant reading.

ENEMY – All Coy positions, with exception of C Coy, now occupied by enemy AFVs and troop carriers moving round both flanks – enemy in strong force in rear – Information from a prisoner, and borne out by observation, put down enemy forces as one mechanized division – Enemy tanks & guns in position around Bn HQ – Enemy aircraft active.

OUR TROOPS:

1/8 Lancs Fus:	No firing from their area – completely out of touch.
1/Royal Scots:	Still in action on right, but enemy between them and us.
2/N – as follows:	A Coy – Reduced to 1 officer & 6 ORs – driven back to Bn HQ.
B Coy –	Totally annihilated since morning.
C Coy –	Apparently still in position but battle had swung round them & they had no influence on events. Possible numbers remaining 50.
D Coy –	No news. Apparently obliterated.

HQ & HQ Coy –	Bn HQ surrounded entirely by tanks, guns & infantry – Total force at HQ inclusive of all details approx 40. Ammunition very low. 1 A/T rifle – 3 LMGs – 'Blue' posts driven in – 'Red' posts only remaining.
CARRIERS:	No news.
MORTARS:	Annihilated.

NOTE:
C Coy, although numerically strong enough to be of use, were completely isolated, and were completely outside the main movement of events – No means of communication existed – the enemy was strongly interposed between themselves and us. Apparently the enemy decided to simply hold the Coy in a state of inaction and after reducing other centres of resistance dealt with C Coy at their leisure.

The Battalion's strength, including the fifty in 'C' Company was estimated at 100 all ranks.

German units still moving to the rear of Duriez Farm provided good targets, but there were now far too many targets for the available ammunition. The supply was almost exhausted. Captain Hastings had collected rounds from the rifles and pouches of the wounded. Bren gun magazines had also been broken up and the bullets, which were the same calibre, .303, as the rifles, were distributed. Every shot had to count; in the words of the orders issued: 'Fire only when certain of results.'

At 1640, a message was received from Brigade. Long observed:

Message at low strength, obviously from a greater distance than formerly – Message stated 'You are to hold on till dusk. If possible and if any of you are left you may withdraw to N.E. to La Nouvelle France – cross water – you will then be met and guided.' Bde assured we would hold on – Bde told we could not transmit these orders to 1/RS & Lancs Fus: attempt was made to get in touch with 1/RS – This failed.

The War Diary of 4th Infantry Brigade tells it slightly differently. Earlier in the afternoon, at 1300 hrs, 2nd Division had issued a 'permissive order' to Brigadier Warren for withdrawal, but no rendezvous was initially given. 'Little or no hope of an organized withdrawal in daylight but at 1445 hrs an RV – La Nouvelle France – was received and communicated to 2/Norfolks who agreed that no withdrawal was possible till dark.' They were asked to pass this information to the Royal Scots 'but it was doubtful whether until it was dark, this could be done'.

Major Ryder called a conference of all his available officers: Major Richardson, Captain Long, Lieutenant Woodwark, Second Lieutenant Willeson, who was wounded but still able to walk, and Captain Hastings. Ryder suggested that, as darkness fell, parties of men, each accompanied by an officer, should attempt to crawl out of Duriez Farm.

In reality it was a forlorn hope. Any attempt at escape would be one last gesture of defiance. The end was near. The long May days meant that darkness was several hours away and it would certainly not take the Germans much longer to overwhelm the farm. Ryder conceded by stating that it would be unlikely that any could get away. He knew that he would have to give the few remaining men under his command a stark choice.

Several more shells slammed into HQ, shaking the walls and showering those inside with more brick dust and plaster. Brigade, according to Long, was informed that it was unlikely they could now last until dusk and their wireless was about to be destroyed.

The Brigade War Diary records 'the last courageous message' from Major Ryder was received 'at 1530 hrs'. He told the Brigade Major that their Battalion HQ was on fire 'and that their wireless was in the cellar and could not be got out and they were going to break it up'. The Regiment was fighting on its own ground surrounded. Ryder's final words were that 'he would bring his Bn to the RV given after dark. From that moment no further news.'

The wireless was destroyed. The remaining battalion paperwork, including the War Diary, which Captain Hastings had tied up in a sack, was taken into the courtyard and thrown into the pond. At first the sack floated so Hastings threw a bicycle onto it to make sure that it sank.[10]

All equipment now surplus to requirements which could be of

use to the Germans was destroyed. Those who had run out of ammunition smashed their rifles, some of which ended up in the pond. The one item of motor transport left, a truck, was set on fire; so, too, was the remaining petrol, but not all of it was destroyed and some did fall into enemy hands.

With the farmhouse burning and the roof in danger of collapsing, Ryder ordered everybody out.

Signaller William O'Callaghan made for the byre which was about 25 yards away. With bullets whining around him, it was the fastest he ever covered that distance in his entire life. In order to reach the door of the byre he had to run round the corner of the pond and he remembered seeing the butts and barrels of smashed rifles sticking out of the water.[11]

Two of the shell bursts had wounded Captain Long and Lieutenant Woodwark. Stunned, they had managed to scramble to their feet and stumble out of the stricken farmhouse. On returning to his post, Long realized that his head was bleeding. Major Ryder bandaged the wound but soon after he had left the scene, Long collapsed and was unconscious for about twenty-five minutes.

Although it was initially thought that all personnel had been evacuated from the farmhouse, both Major Richardson and Second Lieutenant Willeson were missing. It could only be assumed that they had been killed when the roof collapsed.

The byre where O'Callaghan had sought refuge was built of brick and measured 33 feet in length by 21 feet wide. There were about forty men there when he first arrived. Cyril Jolly wrote:

> O'Callaghan had left his pack in this cowhouse when they first came to the farm. He had stowed it in a manger and, as he stood against the wall regaining his breath, he remembered that there were several hundred packs of cigarettes in his pack. These cigarettes were part of the remains of a N.A.A.F.I. store. A dispatch rider had found it and returned to his unit with thousands of English cigarettes which he had shared among the Signals Section. When O'Callaghan recalled the precious contents of his kit, the thought of losing them all so disturbed him that he decided he would try and stow as many as he could about his person. That thought saved his life, for, as he moved from the wall towards the manger, a mortar shell penetrated

the brickwork in the very place where he had stood. Another soldier had moved a pace or so to lean against the wall where O'Callaghan had been and the shell took him full in the back.[12]

The time had come for a final decision, one that Ryder was prepared to leave to his men. It appears that he had earlier gone round the farm seeking opinions on whether they should fight on or surrender. Reaction was mixed: some said they should surrender; others, like Signaller Bob Brown, were for fighting on because he felt:

> the morale was very high. There was no thought of being taken prisoner, getting killed or wounded. We were just carrying on fighting, carrying on the defence and making a joke of it all really. Laughing and joking between each other . . . Eventually he [Ryder] said that it was no good wasting human life. We couldn't hold them up indefinitely. We'd held them up for three days on the canal which was very good effort and he'd decided that we should cease firing. But he said that if anybody thought they could get away, then we were entitled to do our own thing. We wouldn't be running away from the battalion. We would be trying to save ourselves.

In the byre, Ryder, for the last time, asked the battered remnants of his battalion whether they should fight on or surrender. For his part he was not ordering them one way or the other. He was giving no more orders. He would accept their decision.

Again reaction was mixed but when it was put to a show of hands, the majority of the men chose surrender.

All they could find for a flag was a dirty white towel which was tied to a rifle. Opening the door a fraction, the makeshift flag was displayed until the Germans stopped firing. But the first group of men, led by a Sergeant Major, had only walked a few paces when they were fired on by a machine-gun. Several were cut down. The survivors turned back but found their way into the byre blocked by those crowding in the doorway to see what was happening. In the mêlée the men seemed to be on the verge of panic, until one of the officers took control and the door was closed.[13]

Tense minutes passed. They decided to try again. This time there were no shots fired as the sad procession of dishevelled, exhausted, khaki-clad figures, hands above their heads, made their way onto the bright sunlit meadow. For them, battered but alive, the war had ended.

Notes

1. Sebag-Montefiore, *Dunkirk*, Hallett.
2. German accounts are drawn from the Le Paradis War Crimes Investigation and Trial, 1948. A full verbatim test of the trial and investigative reports are held at the Royal Norfolk Regimental Museum, Norwich.
3. Sebag-Montefiore, *Dunkirk*, Hallett.
4. Bob Brown quoted in Sebag-Montefiore.
5. Sebag-Montefiore, *Dunkirk*, Hallett.
6. Imperial War Museum, Sound Archive; Arthur Brough's interview, accession number 16972.
7. Jolly, *The Vengeance of Private Pooley*.
8. Ripley, *Hitler's Praetorians*.
9. Sebag-Montefiore, *Dunkirk*, Hastings.
10. *Ibid.*
11. Jolly, *The Vengeance of Private Pooley*.
12. *Ibid.*
13. *Ibid.*

CHAPTER 10

'Operation Dynamo now complete.'

Two MILES TO THE SOUTH, the fifty or so remaining men of 'C' Company were ready to fight on. With communications between their Company HQ at Locon and Duriez Farm cut, Acting Major Elwes had no way of knowing what was happening at Le Paradis. Sending a runner for information would be suicidal, so all he could do was to try and follow the last firm order he knew of, that issued by the Brigadier to fight to the 'last man, last round'.

During the night, Elwes withdrew all his men to Company HQ, a substantially built farmhouse which provided a strong defensive position and a relatively safe shelter for the wounded in the cellars. The ammunition supply was good but they were completely isolated. It appears that Captain Long's assessment of their situation was correct. 'C' Company's position had been surrounded and the German intention was to deal with them later, some time after Le Paradis had fallen.

At about the time Major Ryder surrendered, Captain Long regained consciousness. He was lying in a ditch which ran beside the road on the southern side of the farmhouse and he said that the time was 1715. Lieutenant David Draffin, the Medical Officer, was there, so, too, was Captain Hastings and two or three other men. A white towel was produced and Hastings held it above his head until the firing ceased.

'Two of my men pulled me from the ditch,' recalled Long. 'The Germans were there with Tommy guns.'

They were told to wait by the road. When they had been joined by twenty-five to thirty other captives, they were marched off in an easterly direction to the crossroads in Le Paradis.

Long had only one complaint about the treatment of prisoners. That night heavy rain fell and wounded men were left outside throughout. He asked if they could be taken inside but was told that it was impossible. Otherwise, the general demeanour of the German Company Commander and his men towards their prisoners was as good as could be expected under the conditions, and certainly in accordance with the rules of war. One German soldier gave Captain Long some biscuits, another some chocolate which he shared with his men.

The German officer gave Long permission to go onto the battle-field to look for any wounded men who had not yet been picked up. He could take with him six men, either unguarded on parole, or without parole but guarded. Accompanied by one guard, the party went out and brought back two wounded.

The same officer then took Long to the German Officers' Mess for a meal. During their conversation, the German asked if it was true that the British had been told to shoot all captured SS troops because they were considered to be civilians rather than soldiers. This, of course, was denied.[1]

The German also revealed that his particular SS unit was from Danzig. This suggests that they were the SS Heimwehr *Danzig*, formerly a home defence force stationed in the demilitarized Free City of Danzig. This unit was affiliated to the SS Totenkopfverbände and subsequently absorbed into the Totenkopf Division. Their record during the Polish campaign was brutal. A unit of Polish troops defending a post office in Danzig had been massacred in cold blood by the SS Heimwehr *Danzig* after surren-dering. On 8 September 1939, thirty-three Polish civilians had been shot by these SS troops in the village of Ksaizki in the province of Pomerania. It is ironic that if this was the same unit, it was treating its British prisoners in accordance with the principles laid down in the Geneva Convention.

As dawn broke on 28 May, German troop carriers closed in on 'C' Company's HQ at Locon. Acting Major Elwes, still determined to carry out the last-known order, led an attack on the advancing vehicles but was killed. In order to save further unnecessary casu-alties, Second Lieutenant Simpson surrendered. The Company's strength was forty.

During the morning Captain Long and the contingent of

prisoners were marched to Locon. There, in a barn, he made a rough count of the survivors: approximately seventy officers and men. Among them were Captain Hastings, Lieutenant Draffin and Captain Gordon, who had been brought in with the remnants of the 1st Royal Scots.

While the captured survivors waited at Locon, a few of their fellow Norfolks were struggling their way northwards towards the coast. When the final assault on the Canal Line had begun at dawn on the previous day, the men of B Echelon had been told to move out. But where were they to go? At first nobody had any idea; instructions were vague. Their progress was slow, the roads clogged with refugees. As Walter Gilding explained:

> It was basically just the cook element who had the cooks' trucks and the quartermaster with his stores truck that were trying to get back wherever – we didn't even know about Dunkirk then. All we were informed was that we were going back to another rendezvous. It was absolute chaos. Five miles would take half a day. If the Stukas came down we would dive off the lorries and get into the hedgerows or ditches and the refugees would do the same. They wouldn't be so quick off the mark as us, so we would pile back into the lorry and drive through before the refugees assembled on the roadways again. But you wouldn't go far before you came unstuck again and they'd all be on the road again with their handcarts, baggage, horse and carts; you name it, everything was there. By this time we had got split up. With the refugee problem it was difficult to keep two or three vehicles together.

After a couple of days of painfully slow progress, during which Gilding estimated they covered between 15 and 20 miles, they decided to abandon the truck. Walking appeared to be the speedier option. Before continuing, however, the lorry had to be rendered useless, which the driver did by draining the sump and running the engine until it seized. The vehicle was then pushed into a road-side canal, which was already serving as a graveyard for other immobilized relics of BEF transport.

Setting off on foot, their journey, which had started without any idea of a destination, now had an objective: Dunkirk, they had heard, was the port from which British troops were being evacuated. Stragglers from other units, seeking some form of leadership, saw that this group of Norfolks were being led by a sergeant and immediately fell in with them. They reached Dunkirk on Thursday, 30 May. Gilding recalled:

> It was chaotic, buildings were smoking, smouldering, there was ruins. The church was standing there, all the front of it pitted with bomb splinters and bullets . . . We arrived at one end of the beach where all the sand dunes were. There was a beachmaster, a naval officer, directing the lads on the beaches. He said, 'New arrivals, Sergeant, just take them to the far end of the sand dunes and dig in facing the other way.' We had ten rifles and I think everyone had some ammunition. We went to the allocated place and dug in. We stayed there that night which would be the 30th/31st. We had a bird's eye view from where we were; watching all the lads lining up down to the water's edge ready to be evacuated, with gaps of twenty to thirty yards between each group. There must have been ten of these queues. Out in the water, way out on the horizon, were naval destroyers and also civilian boats: private yachts and all types of boats. Plying in between the beach and them were small boats, some just rowing boats. I thought, 'God, they're going to take a long while to get this lot off!' An oil depot had been bombed. It was burning and the smoke was blowing across the beach, which was a Godsend really, because it was more or less a camouflage and the Germans couldn't see the beaches themselves. I thought, 'Well there's no way we're going to hold up the whole German Army! It's just a matter of time. We shall be either overrun, captured or hopefully we're going to be evacuated!'

During the early hours of Saturday, 1 June, Sergeant Gilding was instructed to take his group to the water's edge. The next boat was theirs.

> By this time there were very few on the beach. One boat came in that couldn't get in because it was too shallow. The second or third boat that came in must have been flat bottomed, and

we all piled on to it but found that it wouldn't take off because it was stuck on the sands. Several of us had to get out and push it until we could float. Then we were taken out to a larger vessel which was a Belgian pleasure boat. I was pulled over the side, shown down into the cabin. It held about four people and there were about twenty of us in there. Some of them just had to stand; there was no room to even sit down. We were given some blankets and a hot drink. For myself and several others we just dropped off to sleep jammed in that cabin. I was told, but I didn't know anything about it, that we were machine-gunned on the way out. I hadn't had any sleep, except catnaps; you sort of shut your eyes wandering along half asleep, since we left Le Paradis. I woke when we arrived at Dover, somebody said, 'Come on lads, we're here, you're in England!'

When we went ashore I thought everybody was going to shoot us, especially being a regular soldier. We'd run away, that was the feeling I had. But instead of that there were people cheering and clapping us as if we were heroes; giving us mugs of tea and sandwiches. We looked a sorry sight I think – like scruffy soldiers.

Three days later, at 1423 on 4 June, the message was sent out from the Admiralty: 'Operation Dynamo now complete.' In all, 338,226 men had been evacuated from the mole at Dunkirk and the wide sandy beaches stretching away for over 10 miles to De Panne in Belgium. Of the soldiers rescued, 198,315 were British; 139,911 were Allied, mostly French.

On 4 June, Winston Churchill addressed the House of Commons. He had fully expected to announce 'the greatest military disaster in our long history'. In a speech lasting around thirty-four minutes, he said that he thought around 20,000 to 30,000 might have been evacuated, the remainder of the army lost. But many more had been saved enough on which to build the armies of the future.

'Now, suddenly, the scene is clear,' he said. 'A miracle of deliverance has been achieved by valour, perseverance, perfect discipline and faultless service.'

In the pages of the newspapers and over the airwaves, defeat became a victory of sorts; fiction was interwoven with the facts. Spin, as we would call it today, dubbed the evacuation as 'one of the most wonderful episodes in our history'. The BBC said that the British Expeditionary Force had 'come back to glory'.

History itself never changes, but our knowledge and therefore our interpretation of it does. As the truth about Dunkirk has been stripped of its apocryphal embellishments, as new material has been brought to light, historians have been able to tell it as it happened; in the words of that hackneyed old phrase, 'warts and all'. Some have tended to emphasize those warts, and indeed there were many, but they must be balanced by those who gave their all. Those regiments like the Royal Norfolks who manned the Canal Line and other strongpoints, trying to hold open that precious corridor just long enough for others to escape. The Holy Boys fought almost to the last. Of the 2nd Division's strength on 30–31 May, it was written in the Official History that 'only a composite company formed of men of the 5th Brigade was left.' The Division had gone into battle fielding nine infantry battalions; three field regiments and one anti-tank regiment of the Royal Artillery; and three field companies and one field park company of the Royal Engineers; in terms of manpower approximately 13,800. The 4th Infantry Brigade, according to its War Diary entry on 31 May, had started out with about ninety officers and 2,500 other ranks; of these only about 650 returned.

On the day Operation Dynamo ended, the 2nd Battalion Royal Norfolk Regiment began the process of rebuilding. Forty-nine men under Lieutenant Grant were sent from Bradford to Folkestone and formed the basis of the new battalion. Grant, formerly the Quartermaster, was one of the survivors who had escaped from France with the other men of B Echelon.

Twenty more men under Second Lieutenant Fulton joined them from Aldershot on 5 June. Fulton, too, had made it back to Britain, having been attached to Brigade as Brigade LO. Next day, Major Wood arrived from ITC, Norwich, to assume command.

By the evening of 7 June, the Battalion's strength was five officers and 134 men. Two of the officers, Captain Straghan MC and Second Lieutenant Hatch MC, had been with the 4th Infantry Brigade's Anti-Tank Company in France; twenty-seven other men had served in France with various HQ units.

Two days later, the Holy Boys moved back to Bradford where they joined the 1st Royal Scots and 1st/8th Lancashire Fusiliers, who were likewise rebuilding, at Belle Vue Barracks. Captain Allen, another survivor, was already there with the HQ of 4th Infantry Brigade. During the afternoon, two more survivors, Second Lieutenant Jones, who had been in charge of the Carrier Platoon, and Second Lieutenant Swainson reported to the Battalion.

Conscripts from the Infantry Training Centres, having completed their six months basic training, were initially upset by the dishevelled appearance of those men who had made it back from France.

'We were a little surprised,' said Private Dennis Boast of the Carrier Platoon,[2] 'that this was the regular army just turned up and not looking in very good shape. But that was very unfair of us.'

That many of the originals had been left behind was brought home to the replacements, one day, when the mail arrived.

'There were several of them standing round,' Corporal Bill Seymour explained,[3] 'and the post Sergeant was sorting out the sacks of mail. As he was pulling out letters from the mail bags, they were saying such things as, "No, he copped it! No, he copped it! He's back!" . . . It sounded very bad.'

By 12 June, when the Duke of Gloucester visited the Brigade, the Norfolks' strength had risen to eight officers and 206 other ranks.

On 15 June, Brigadier Warren issued a brigade order, in which he paid a warm tribute to the men under his command:

> You have acquitted yourselves as I expected you would do, with devotion, with courage, and in keeping with the very highest traditions of the Regiments to which you belong. When history comes to be written, it will be recorded that the part played by the 4th Infantry Brigade was second to none in valour, dauntless courage and tenacity. Its refusal to give an inch to the enemy contributed tremendously to the successful withdrawal of the 330,000 British and French troops to this country. It was an optimistic hope that perhaps 30,000 might be got away; 300,000 was considered an impossibility, but deeds such as yours made the impossible possible.[4]

One man who epitomized that dauntless courage died in the early hours of the following morning at the Royal Sussex County

General Hospital in Brighton. Company Sergeant Major George Gristock was one of two Norfolks who were being treated at the hospital after being wounded during the fighting on the Escaut. The other man was Ernie Leggett, who had been admitted on 28 May and was to remain there for nearly a year. A few days after his admission, while recovering from an operation, he received an unexpected order:

> The sister of the ward came to me and she said, 'There's somebody in the next ward who has ordered that he should see you!' I said, 'Well, who is it?' She said, 'Wait and see when you get in there!' They had to lift me out, put me on a wheel chair, they wheeled me in and I was greeted with, 'Hello, boy, how are you?' It was Sergeant Major Gristock! I saw the cage over his legs and he told me his legs had been so shot up by the broadside of this machine-gun that they had to amputate his legs from the hip. I noticed that on his bed rail was a line of about ten or twelve bottles of ale. And it immediately went through my mind that a man in such a condition as he was in, if they allowed him to drink, then he must be in a very poor way. He said, 'Do something for me, boy.' I said, 'Yes, what's that?' He said, 'Fill this up for me!' He couldn't do it himself, he had to be fed and everything. He'd got one of these things like a little teapot with a handle on the end. I filled it with beer and held it to his mouth and he just supped this bottle of ale. He said, 'Cor, pour another one in!' I did that and I did that every day I went through to see him. I told him, 'I saw what you did.' He said, 'Yes, the bastards, but I wiped them out, I got the so and sos!' To me he seemed as if he was getting better. We talked in army parlance about the old days; how we'd played football matches and sport . . . I used to stay with him for half an hour or an hour. Every day they'd wheel me through. Then that horrible morning came on 16th June when they hadn't come and got me. I said to the nurse, 'Nurse, take me through to see my Sergeant Major!' She said, 'No, sorry . . .'

George Gristock, who had enlisted into the Dragoon Guards in 1919 and transferred to the Norfolks in 1935, was thirty-nine. He died not knowing that he was to be awarded the Victoria Cross for his act of valour on the Escaut. The citation appeared in the *London Gazette* on 23 August 1940.

Captain Barclay later recalled that during the early weeks of the war, his appointment of Gristock as Sergeant Major in one of 'A' Company's platoons led to a clash between Barclay and his Commanding Officer.

'I had a hell of a row with him. I said I wouldn't change my mind and the CO didn't speak to me for a couple of days.' Barclay's judgment and single-mindedness had been vindicated.

Gristock's father and his sister, who was a member of the Auxiliary Transport Service, attended the investiture at Buckingham Palace and received the medal from King George VI.

His body rests in the cemetery at Brighton, on a hill overlooking the sea. His headstone, in the familiar form of the Commonwealth War Graves Commission, has a carving of the Victoria Cross and the inscription: 'In Loving Memory of My Dear Son. Gone But Not Forgotten.'

Notes

1. The first few hours of Captain Long's captivity are based on his evidence given during the Le Paradis War Crimes Trial in 1948.
2. Imperial War Museum, Sound Archive; Dennis Boast's interview, accession number 17535.
3. Imperial War Museum, Sound Archive; Bill Seymour's interview, accession number 17672.
4. Quoted in Kemp, *History of the Royal Norfolk Regiment.*

CHAPTER 11

'If I ever get out of here the swine who did this will pay for it.'

TEN DAYS AFTER THE NORFOLKS had surrendered at Le Paradis, two wounded soldiers were brought to the Béthune Civil Hospital. Private Albert Pooley and Signaller William O'Callaghan had spent much of that time hiding in a pigsty after surviving the cold-blooded shooting of ninety-seven of their comrades. Many of them were those who, with Major Ryder, had left the byre at Duriez Farm under a white flag of surrender. Others, captured in the churchyard at Le Paradis and in nearby houses, brought the total to ninety-nine. Not all of them were Holy Boys; a few came from other units.

They were paraded on the Rue du Paradis then marched off through fields keeping parallel to the road. On reaching a field some 500 to 800 yards from Duriez Farm, they were halted and searched. The treatment meted out to them was brutal. They were pushed, kicked and struck with rifle butts and pistols. O'Callaghan received a heavy blow to his head for forgetting to hand over his knife when asked if he had any weapons. Another soldier was asked by a guard if he wanted one of the cigarettes which had been thrown on the ground. As the unfortunate man stepped forward and bent down to pick one up, the German smashed his rifle butt into the soldier's face.

'Anybody who was speaking or moving or looking round would be struck,' said Albert Pooley. 'I myself was struck by a German soldier with his rifle. He took 20 cigarettes out of my pocket. I turned to look at him; he struck me with his rifle and knocked me right through the ranks.'[1] Four of his teeth were knocked out by the blow.

Leaving all their kit and personal possessions lying in the field,

157

the prisoners were marched onto the road in column of threes. A long, virtually unbroken line of German transport had halted and the prisoners were subjected to more harsh treatment. None of the German troops responsible was reprimanded. On reaching the farm belonging to Monsieur Louis Creton, they turned off the dusty road into a pasture. The left-hand side of this pasture was bounded by the farmhouse and a long red-brick barn with a steep-pitched pantile roof. Pooley remembered:

> Before I turned into that gateway, I saw, with one of the nastiest feelings I've ever had in my life, two heavy machine-guns inside the meadow. They were manned and pointing at the head of our column! I felt as though an icy hand gripped my stomach. The guns began to spit fire and even as the front men began to fall I said fiercely, 'This can't be. They can't do this to us!'
>
> For a few seconds the cries and shrieks of our stricken men drowned the cracking of the guns. Men fell like grass before a scythe. The invisible blade came nearer and then swept through me. I felt a terrific searing pain in my leg and wrist and pitched forward engulfed in a red world of tearing agony. My scream of pain mingled with the cries of my mates but even as I fell forward into a heap of dying men the thought stabbed my brain, 'If I ever get out of here the swine who did this will pay for it.'[2]

Two hundred rounds had been fired into the columns of unarmed men by two machine-guns from No. 4 Machine-gun Company. Those who had not been killed instantly were dispatched by bayonet, pistol or rifle shots. Corporal Max Schneider, a mortar layer who had been posted to No. 4 Machine-gun Company, said that when he heard the firing he looked over the hedge and saw the British soldiers being mown down. One seriously wounded soldier, who Schneider described as an elderly man (possibly a reference to Major Ryder), raised himself on his elbow and pointed to his heart as if asking for the *coup de grâce*.[3]

Miraculously, within that jumbled heap of bodies two men were still alive. William O'Callaghan had been hit in the arm but Albert Pooley had suffered four wounds to the same leg – two from the initial burst of fire, which may have ricocheted off the barn wall, and two more from subsequent shots as the Germans tried to ensure that nobody would live to tell the tale. What also may have contributed to their survival was that the victims all fell into a depression in the ground.

After dark, in pouring rain, the two men succeeded in freeing themselves from beneath the bodies of their fallen comrades. With Germans sheltering in the barn, they knew they had to get away from that paddock and hide elsewhere, otherwise they were bound to be summarily executed as potential witnesses to a war crime.

As Pooley was unable to walk, O'Callaghan dragged him out of the pasture, across a ditch and through a cornfield until they came upon the buildings of a neighbouring farm owned by Monsieur Duquenne Creton, the brother of Louis.

They took refuge in a Dutch barn but when daylight came and a party of Germans entered the farmyard, they realized that they were in a vulnerable position. They moved to a woodpile for a time until O'Callaghan discovered a pigsty where he made Pooley as comfortable as possible. Raw potatoes and water scooped from puddles in the farmyard provided sustenance of sorts.

Their presence was discovered by Madame Pauline Duquenne Creton when she returned to look at her ruined farmhouse. Her husband was away fighting in the French Army. Accompanied by her eleven-year-old son Victor, she brought food for the two fugitives and did what she could for Pooley's wounds. She knew nothing of the ordeal they had been through, believing that they had been wounded during the fighting and had sought shelter in her pigsty.

They could not remain there indefinitely, however. Pooley's wounds were in need of proper medical attention otherwise loss of his leg or death would occur if infection was allowed to spread. They were also aware of the considerable risk Madame Duquenne Creton was running in helping wounded British soldiers without reporting their whereabouts to the Germans.

Pooley and O'Callaghan succeeded in giving themselves up without implicating their Good Samaritan and were taken to the Béthune Civil Hospital. No questions were asked but the date of their admission was falsely given as 27 May 1940.

There were around ten other wounded Holy Boys in the hospital, including Company Sergeant Major Cockaday and one of the officers. O'Callaghan said that it was the Transport Officer which suggests Captain Hallett, who had been in charge of transport until 26 May, when Major Ryder redistributed his officers and placed Hallett in charge of the remnants of 'B' Company. Second Lieutenant Merritt had taken over the transport and was evacuated to England. Hallett had been wounded and taken prisoner at Le Cornet Malo on 27 May. Hallett's presence gave O'Callaghan the opportunity to report the atrocity at Le Paradis and he decided to do so, but as described by Cyril Jolly:

> The officer made no bones of his disbelief and told O'Callaghan there and then that he did not believe that the Germans would do such a thing . . . O'Callaghan was naturally pretty sore at this open disbelief and told the officer that he could please himself whether he believed it or not, but that he did not make such things up, and that there would be no point in doing so. The officer went down soon after to see Pooley. His arm was in a sling. He sat down on Pooley's bed and demanded, 'What's this cock and bull story O'Callaghan had been telling us about the Germans shooting ninety of our men?'
>
> Pooley was not in a fit state for much interrogation, but he answered, 'It's not a cock and bull story. It's the truth. All the survivors of the Battalion were taken out of Headquarters and machine-gunned.'
>
> 'What happened to the Commanding Officer?'
>
> 'He got it as well,' replied the wounded man.
>
> But the officer, unconvinced, said, 'The Germans would not do such a thing,' and unwilling to worry Pooley any further, turned away.[4]

Sergeant Wright, who knew both Pooley and O'Callaghan well, was also in the hospital recovering from a shoulder wound. He later admitted that he found their story difficult to believe as it simply did not tally with his experience – he and the other survivors of 'C' Company had been treated well following their surrender on 28 May.

If their own side wouldn't believe the story, the incident certainly created something of a stir within the German ranks, even though the culpable unit was part of an SS Division.

Emile Stuerzbecher, the former Adjutant of Totenkopf 2, said that his HQ became aware of what had happened in No. 3 Company's sector towards the end of the day on 27 May. Captain Knoechlein had been so enraged by the heavy losses inflicted on his men, and some allegedly unlawful fighting methods employed by the British, that he had ordered the shooting of the prisoners. The Regiment's Battalion Commander summoned Knoechlein to appear before him, for what was said to have been a stormy interview. Afterwards he told Stuerzbecher, 'These stories that have been going around are correct. Some frightfully dirty work has been going on in No. 3 Company. Knoechlein is a blackguard and a showman but no soldier. He actually maintains he is in the right. There was never anything like it in the World War [i.e. 1914–1918] and the whole thing springs from the mad ideas of the Führer. In any case, this swinish trick spoils the day's success for me.'

Amongst a group of junior officers, feelings ran so high that one of them named Unsald, No. 2 Adjutant to the Battalion Commander, suggested that Knoechlein should be challenged to a duel for the sake of the Regiment's honour. Unsald was, according to Stuerzbecher, a particularly honourable man and his honour in connection with the Regiment would be injured because of that. He was subsequently killed while serving on the Russian front.[5]

On the day after the massacre, Major Freiherr von Riedereer, an officer on the General Staff, discovered the bodies at the Creton Farm, although he stated that the location was in the south-east part of Le Cornet Malo. He at once sent a report to General Command at the HQ of XVI Army Corps, as follows:

Close examination showed that it was apparently a case of prisoners who had been shot, by way of summary execution, in the head; which shots must have been fired at very close range. In some cases the whole skull was smashed, a type of wound which can only have been inflicted by blows from rifle butts or similar weapons. A number of cartridge cases and rifle and pistol ammunition were lying in the vicinity.

I ordered my driver to count the corpses. He reported 89.[6]

On receipt of Riedereer's report, Army Corps HQ immediately asked for a report from the SS Totenkopf. At the same time a Medical Officer was instructed to carry out an examination of the bodies. Dr Haddenhorst who held the rank of Major, reported as follows:

> On the orders of the HQ Staff, I have today 29.5.40 at 1700 hours seen the corpses of about ninety English soldiers . . . ten metres from the long house wall . . . In the ditch on the left hand side of the road that led past the house about five more corpses lay in the water, and in the field which bordered on the left were another four corpses. A medical Co. of the S.S. on the orders of the Div. were engaged in ascertaining the details of the dead and burying the corpses in a mass grave.
>
> The bulk of the corpses lying together in heaps immediately gave the impression of a mass shooting. Upon examination of the individual wounds it was ascertained that they were mostly head wounds caused by rifle ammunition resulting in the blowing off of the cranium and exudation of the brains. Some of the shots were fired from behind. Many of the dead showed several wounds and some of them also had wounds in the back. A few corpses had pistol shots from close range, which is taken as meaning they were the *coup de grâce.*
>
> In a stable attached to the house there were fourteen wounded. They were attended by an M.O. Co. and later removed; when questioned he said that they had been wounded at another spot and carried into the house by German soldiers.[7]

In the meantime, the Totenkopf had started their own investigation. Gunter d'Alquen, a journalist who was serving with a War Correspondents Company, had visited the Totenkopf Divisional Headquarters at Chocques (just west of Béthune) on 27 May. At around noon the following day, while standing near some vehicles awaiting the departure of HQ to a new location, he was approached by Dr Thum, a divisional officer and deputy legal advisor to the Totenkopf. He asked d'Alquen to accompany him on a short journey by car.

Dr Thum explained that British soldiers had been shot by the side of the road. A senior army officer (Major Riedereer) had seen the bodies and the Totenkopf had been asked to investigate. That was the reason for their journey. When the correspondent asked for an explanation of the shooting, Dr Thum said that British soldiers had displayed a white flag with a swastika on it. This had lured German soldiers into the open where they had been subjected to heavy fire causing several casualties.

After losing their way and having to ask directions, they eventually reached 'a small farm situated at right angles to a medium-sized country road. It was possible to look into the backyard from the road.' D'Alquen estimated that about fifty bodies:

> in British uniform were lying in this yard near the building. They were lying in such a position that one can assume they were killed by machine-gun bursts. It struck me at once that the dead soldiers were not wearing helmets, nor did they have equipment with them. I took pictures of the dead bodies and the whole farm. At Thum's request these were to be placed at the disposal of the Division.

Dr Thum then left the farm for a while and when he reappeared he told d'Alquen that 'in a field from which he had returned the equipment of the shot British soldiers was lying in a heap, from which he had come to the conclusion that a summary trial had taken place there.'[8]

The response written on 29 May at 1055 hrs by the Battle HQ of Totenkopf 2 was regarded by Army Corps Command as unsatisfactory and insolent. They accused the English of using dumdum bullets which they stated was proven by their wounded and by the evidence of their officers. They also claimed that a flag bearing a swastika was displayed by the British, luring their soldiers from cover whereupon they were ambushed and wiped out by machine-gun fire. They then gave casualty figures for the fighting at Le Cornet Malo: four officers and 153 NCOs and men killed; eighteen officers and 483 other ranks wounded, and fifty-two men missing. Most of the wounds, they claimed, were in the back. 'It was in our interest to take our revenge for the treacherous and villainous fighting tactics adopted by the English by shooting the remainder of those who took part in the cowardly ambush following a court martial. Reports which give a different account of what happened are malicious and false.'⁹

In the course of a few typewritten lines, the Totenkopf were trying to portray themselves as victims, their heavy losses not due to the recklessness of their Divisional Commander, Theodor Eicke, and his utter contempt for human life, nor his Division's inexperience of all-out warfare. La Bassée was the first major action for the SS regiments concerned. They had come up against two British regiments which had a long history of valiant service behind them. In seniority, the Royal Scots were the 1st of Foot, who referred to themselves as 'Pontius Pilate's bodyguard'. The Norfolks were the 9th of Foot and were already 255 years old. All of them were professional soldiers, steeped in the traditions of their forbears. They had been told to hold their sector for as long as possible and the depleted ranks did just that, with a dogged determination which was an effrontery to the arrogant pride of the SS. How could so few hold up so many for so long without resorting to foul means? The Totenkopf regarded itself as an élite, superior to the *Wehrmacht* and above criticism.

Corps HQ, however, was not impressed. At 1130 on 29 May, instructions were issued for the Totenkopf to answer the following list of questions:

1. On whose orders was the standing court on the prisoners convened?

2. How was the standing court convened?

3. Who confirmed the sentence and ordered the execution?

4. Place and time of execution and how this was carried out?

5. How many prisoners were shot?

6. On how many prisoners were dumdum bullets found?

7. How many SS men were hit by dumdum bullets and how was this fact recognizable?

8. Where and in what stage of the fighting was the swastika flag exhibited by the enemy? Who saw it? Was it captured?

9. Why was the fact of such importance, viz: the use of dumdum bullets by the enemy in considerable quantities, not reported immediately via the Intelligence channels and exhibits to prove the charge not provided?

All English shot or killed within the Division limits are to be buried at once in a proper manner. Their identity discs are to be taken off them and together with papers belonging to the dead sent to the burial officer of the HQ 4th Army with details of the location of the grave.[10]

These questions were never answered. On 3 June, Corps HQ wrote to Sixth Army HQ enclosing the various documents:

In spite of requests by telephone and subsequently verbally repeated demands the report was not received by 1.6.40 on which date the [Totenkopf] Div. left the Corps Command area.

The Corps HQ therefore submits the documents now enclosed with the request that they be forwarded to the competent authority. The case appears, especially in view of the number of those killed, so important that an unbiased investigation must be instituted.[11]

No further action was taken but Theodor Eicke appears to have been lucky to retain his command. Berlin heard of the atrocity and Stuerzbecher said that he had almost been dismissed. As a result, Eicke never forgave the Regiment for not reporting the affair directly to him.

In the final analysis, the Totenkopf's operational performance left much to be desired. Although they did not lack courage, their recklessness resulted in heavy losses of both manpower and equipment. Amongst the 1,140 casualties suffered, 300 were officers. As well as an unspecified number of rifles, heavy machine-guns and mortars, forty-six trucks and eight armoured cars were lost. Himmler, apparently, was 'not amused'.[12]

On 2 June, Louis Creton came back to his farm which he had left on 20 May. He recalled that:

On my return I ascertained that a communal grave surmounted by a small cross had been dug in one of the meadows of my farm.

I also noticed bullet marks on the stable wall facing on to the meadow, at man's height. By the wall, bits of brains and pools of congealed blood were scattered on the ground.

At a distance of about twenty-five metres from the wall mentioned I found a pile of about two hundred German cartridge cases. I learnt from Monsieur and Madame Dieu that ninety-seven British soldiers were shot by Germans belonging to the unit which had occupied the village.

In 1942, I was present at the disinterment of the British soldiers, and I noticed that many of the bodies still had bandages on them, either on their arms or head; one of them still wore a dressing on his arm showing that his limb had been fractured.[13]

Cyril Jolly quoted an article which was published in the *Nord Éclair,* and described how the inhabitants of the area tended the mass grave:

People came from Lille, Béthune and Merville to deck the clay mound and the cross that M. Creton had planted there with flowers. Mlls. Jeanne and Madeleine Creton saw continually to the preservation of the tomb. Later, some British flags were tied to the cross.

Some German officers noticed this. The Gestapo came down to the farm, and threatened the whole family with deportation.

In May 1942, at the time of exhumation, the victims were identified and transferred to the communal cemetery of 'Paradis' and their roll of names left at the prefecture of Arras.[14]

Owing to the severity of Pooley's wounds, he was repatriated in October 1943. While at Richmond Convalescent Camp in Yorkshire, he reported the shooting at Le Paradis. Soon after, he was interrogated by two officers whose casual, unbelieving attitude to his story annoyed him immensely. When asked if there was anyone who could corroborate the accusation, Pooley replied in the affirmative but would not divulge the name. O'Callaghan was still a prisoner of war and Pooley was afraid that if the name should be leaked, O'Callaghan might conveniently disappear without trace. Even when one of the officers assured him that he was 'security', Pooley remained firm in his refusal. He had no trust in these two officers and certainly no trust in so-called British security. 'He had learned in German prison camps how dubious some of our security measures had been. Ugly stories had circulated about the Dieppe Raid, and the preparations the Germans had made for the attackers.[15]

When O'Callaghan was released in 1945, he was asked, on his arrival at an airfield in Buckinghamshire, if he had any war crimes to report. He was handed a form, which he immediately completed, giving details of the Le Paradis atrocity. Nothing more was heard – the form just disappeared into the system.

A year passed before the wheels of justice started to turn – not as a result of the form O'Callaghan had filled in, nor Pooley's interrogation at Richmond. The catalyst appears to have been a friend of Pooley's, who, over a drink in a public house, said that the story was too far-fetched to believe. He felt that after all the years of pain that Pooley had been through, he might simply have imagined it. This was the spur that moved Pooley into action. He decided to return to France.

'I wanted to make sure of certain facts,' he said 'and that it was not a dream.'[16]

In 1946, he arrived in Béthune and made his way to an estaminet run by Madame Desruelles who, together with some other locals, had adopted wounded British prisoners while they were recovering in the hospital. Madame Desruelles had provided Pooley with hot coffee, eggs, cigarettes and occasionally British beer. Likewise, Monsieur and Madame Albert Caron had visited Pooley and all were delighted to see him again.

At first he did not tell them the real reason for his visit. He went to Le Paradis and spent some time in the War Cemetery behind the church. At Louis Creton's farm, he prized two bullets out of the barn wall. They were identical to two taken from his leg. He met again Pauline Duquenne Creton and finally revealed to her that he had survived the massacre.

For six years his own countrymen had doubted his story, but this French community knew the truth. Those who had treated him with such kindness in 1940 came to his assistance once more.

Pooley did not tell Madame Desruelles what he had discovered that day in Le Paradis, but Madame Duquenne Creton came to see him and she told all the story. Madame Desruelles was astounded. She was also very hurt that Pooley had not taken her into his confidence, but as he explained to her later, fear of reprisals had sealed his lips in the hospital at Béthune and disbelief and interminable illness had made him doubt his own story. He had not even told his own wife of the massacre and why he had come back to France. When Madame Desruelles heard that his story had been disbelieved she was highly indignant and the French Civil Police were informed.

Meanwhile Madame Creton told the headman of her village what Pooley had revealed to her. He was amazed that the men she had sheltered at her farm were survivors of the atrocity. He immediately communicated with the police, for this was new and strong light on a dark deed that had happened in their midst. The Civil Police passed the information on to the French military authorities. The fire was lit.[17]

The investigation was led by Lieutenant Colonel Alexander Scotland, Commanding Officer of the War Crimes Interrogation Unit at London District Cage. Scotland was furious when told that both Pooley (in 1943) and O'Callaghan (in 1945) had officially reported the shooting. He vowed that heads would roll, but none ever did and neither report was found.

In France, the investigation was assisted by Inspector Henri Gallet of the Béthune Police who interviewed various French witnesses and provided statements and photographs. He had first been alerted to the possibility that a war crime had been committed at Le Paradis by people returning to their homes after the fighting in the area had ceased. He had also heard rumours, at the time, that bodies of dead British soldiers had been robbed.

Lieutenant Colonel Scotland's first task was to pinpoint which German regiments had fought at Le Paradis. Both British Intelligence and captured German Orders of Battle provided the answer: Totenkopf Infantry Regiment 2. Testimony from some former SS soldiers pointed to the man who had commanded No. 3 Company, Fritz Knoechlein. At the time he was a Captain but had finished the war as a Lieutenant Colonel. He had been awarded the Iron Cross in May 1940, the German Cross in 1942 and the Knight's Cross in 1944, these last two decorations being for the campaign in Russia.

One of the most crucial pieces of evidence against him came from Theodor Emke who had been a section commander in the Machine-Gun Platoon which had carried out the execution. He maintained that he was not actually in command of his section at the time, his Platoon Commander, Petri, having taken over. Emke was about fifty paces away from the British prisoners as they marched into the pasture. He described what happened next:

> As the column was within four to five paces of the right corner of the house and the last prisoners had just reached the left corner i.e., the group was completely covering the front of the house, Knoechlein suddenly shouted 'Fire'. Simultaneously, because of this shout, Schroedel and Petri gave the order 'Open fire'. Both guns opened fire immediately. I involuntarily looked. My attention was taken by the prisoners who collapsed from right to left and fell forward. The business was over in a few seconds.

Command of the section was handed back to Emke and he and the gun crews left the scene. After they had walked about a hundred paces, they 'heard some shots from there, which must have been either pistol or rifle shots'. Later that day, Petri told Emke that Knoechlein had given the order for the shooting.

Pooley and O'Callaghan were the principal witnesses. They independently identified Knoechlein, as did, during the trial, an elderly Frenchwoman, Romaine Castel. She was near Louis Creton's farm, less than 100 metres away, when she heard the bursts of machine-gun fire and the cries of distress. When she attempted to leave the area shortly afterwards, she was confronted by a German officer, forced to her knees and threatened with a pistol. He called her a spy and said he was going to kill her. She pleaded for her life and he finally let her go after asking if there were any British troops around.

On 28 August 1948, in No. 5 Court, Curio Haus, Altona, Hamburg, Fritz Knoechlein was indicted:

Pursuant to Regulation 4 of the Regulations for the Trial of War Criminals, [Fritz Knoechlein] is charged with committing a war crime in that he in the vicinity of Paradis, Pas de Calais, France, on or about May 27th, 1940, in violation of the laws and usages of war, was concerned in the killing of about ninety prisoners-of-war, members of The Royal Norfolk Regiment and other British units.

He pleaded not guilty.

The trial began on 11 October. The Court comprised of the President, Lieutenant Colonel E. C. Van der Kiste, of the Essex Regiment, the Judge Advocate, Mr F. Honig, Barrister, and four members: Major P. Witty, Major C. Champion, Captain J.E. Tracey and Captain A. Preston. Counsel for the Prosecution was Mr T. Field-Fisher and Defence Counsel was Dr Uhde.

The trial lasted eleven days. At 1130 on 25 October 1948, Lieutenant Colonel Van der Kiste delivered the verdict:

The Court's finding which I am going to pronounce now, and the sentence which I will announce later on, are both subject to confirmation by a higher authority.

Fritz Knoechlein, stand up. The Court finds you guilty of the crime of which you have been charged.

Dr Uhde, you understand that should your client wish to put in a petition either on the finding or sentence you must put in an application within forty-eight hours and the petition must be within fourteen days.

After hearing favorable testimony from four character witnesses, the court was adjourned. At 1500 hrs it reassembled and Lieutenant Colonel Van der Kiste pronounced the sentence: 'Death by hanging'.

The execution was carried out by the British Garrison in Hamburg on 28 January 1949. Albert Pooley's vow, made while he lay in agony beneath his dead and dying comrades, had been fulfilled.

In the space of forty years, the massacre at Le Paradis has been tainted by the allegation that it was carried out as a reprisal for the massacre of 400 German prisoners during the British counter-attack at Arras. This allegation was also applied to another killing of unarmed British prisoners on 28 May, the day after Le Paradis. At Esquelbecq near Wormhoudt, which lies around 22 miles north of Le Paradis, some eighty men of the Royal Warwickshire Regiment, the Cheshire Regiment and Royal Artillery, were herded into a small barn. They were then killed with bullets and grenades by a battalion of SS Leibstandarte Adolf Hitler Division.

Veterans of the Durham Light Infantry, who had taken part in the Arras operation, told author Nicholas Harman that their unit 'did murder an unknown number of Germans who had surrendered, and were legitimate prisoners of war'. The prisoners had been taken during the advance but when the DLI were forced to retreat they 'could not take the prisoners back with them, so they killed the SS men rather than set them free to fight again'.

Harman published this revelation in his book *Dunkirk: The Necessary Myth*, Hodder & Stoughton, 1980. Subsequently, it appeared in Ronald Atkin's *Pillar of Fire: Dunkirk 1940*, Sidgwick & Jackson, 1990 by, and Angus Calder's *The Myth of the Blitz*, Jonathan Cape, 1991.

Professor Brian Bond, in an essay published in 1997, 'The British Field Army in France and Belgium 1939–40', did refute the accusation made in Harman's book but also said that the 'excuse of the SS units involved was that they were retaliating for British massacres of German prisoners during the fighting around Arras on 21 May'.

No such allegations were made in the aftermath of Le Paradis. Evidence contained in German documents is clear enough. When XVI Army Corps HQ asked for an explanation from the Totenkopf, the only excuse given was the alleged irregular fighting methods employed by the British in that sector: dumdum bullets and the swastika flag. These accusations also formed part of the defence during Fritz Knoechlein's trial.

Max Schneider, under questioning, claimed to have seen the swastika flag hanging from the balcony of a house. The swastika, however, was the wrong way round.

Knoechlein said that at the crossroads in Riez du Vinage, a white piece of material was hung from a window. His men, thinking it was the surrender, approached the house openly only to be fired on.

'My Platoon Commander,' said Knoechlein, 'made a report that the English did not fight according to the laws and usages of war as laid down by the Geneva Convention.'

The unnamed ordnance officer, in a declaration to the War Crimes Investigation Unit, alleged that he saw stretcher-bearers shot while attending the wounded which caused much indignation among the German troops.

When it came to the dumdum bullets, Max Schneider, Walter Fripes and Franz Bachwinkel, all NCOs, claimed to have seen or handled such ammunition. Both Fripes and Bachwinkel said they had submitted reports about it, yet Knoechlein, during his trial, told the court that he had not examined the bullets closely.

Emile Stuerzbecher, however, doubted the genuineness of the ammunition rounds he saw and expressed his doubts to the Battalion Commander. He also told the court that many stories of British irregularities were found to be untrue and arose as a result of excited talk amongst the troops.

August Leitl, a sergeant artificer and ammunition expert, denied that the wounds inflicted on his fallen comrades were caused by dumdum rounds. Most of the dead he collected from the battlefield had large head wounds, but in his opinion the flattening of the bullets was caused by them striking the steel helmets before entering the skull.

Had the Holy Boys been using such ammunition, once they had surrendered the Germans could have convened a court martial. This was made clear in the list of questions sent by Corps HQ to the Totenkopf on 29 May – questions, as we already know, that were never answered. The correct judicial procedure for any such court was clarified by the Judge Advocate, Mr F. Honig, during his summary of evidence towards the end of Knoechlein's trial:

> But for this case it is quite immaterial whether such methods were used or not for Article 2, sub-section 3, of the Geneva Convention states that 'measures of reprisals against prisoners-of-war are forbidden.'
>
> If it was desired to punish prisoners for such methods, proper judicial proceedings should have been taken. Various

provisions must be complied with such as giving the prisoners an opportunity to defend themselves; and a reasonable time must elapse before the death sentence is carried out.

Now there is no evidence, gentlemen, that any of these provisions were observed. Whether or not there was a court – I think I am entitled to say there is no evidence at all that any court sat and judged these prisoners – there is no doubt that the execution was carried out in violation of the laws and usages of war and it automatically becomes a war crime.

In the course of the investigation other instances of war crimes committed by the Totenkopf in the area came to light. The French had discovered the bodies of twenty-one men of the Royal Scots, all of whom had suffered wounds to the neck which was a strong indication that they had been summarily executed after capture.

Sergeant Major Johnstone and the remains of 'A' Company who had fought so valiantly beside the Holy Boys at Le Cornet Malo almost suffered the same fate as Major Ryder and his men. They were lined up and about to be shot when a staff officer of the *Wehrmacht*, who happened to be passing, put a stop to it and actually congratulated the Royal Scots for fighting 'like tigers'.

Three warrant officers were saved from execution by the intervention of Captain Hastings, having been accused of murdering German prisoners. The so-called evidence against them was that they had been captured in a house thought to be a British HQ. Various items of German equipment were found there, but Hastings was able to confirm that the house had not been used as a headquarters by the British.[18]

A German war correspondent was present when an English soldier was shot down in cold blood by an SS man. Signalman Tenius of the War Reporter Platoon said:

in the early hours of May 27th I crossed the Canal d'Aire by the emergency bridge built by S.S. engineers to get to the village of Le Cornet Malo. I was lying behind stacks of corn there to wait for my operational instructions.

After a short while an S.S. man marched along a prisoner, who incidentally had to keep his hands over his head all the way.

I did not bother any more about the prisoner but shortly after I heard a shot coming probably from a pistol. On my asking what had happened I was informed that the captured Englishman had been shot down because he had fired from a house at the S.S.

Later on as I was passing through the stackyard I saw the prisoner lying dead with his face to the ground.[19]

Not all the men in the byre at Duriez Farm became victims of the massacre. Private Bill Carter was initially amongst the doomed group.

'The SS officer claimed we had killed 3,000 Germans,' he recalled, 'and we could see they were very angry. He said we had been using dum dum bullets which expand on impact causing terrible injuries and they said they would kill us. We hadn't been using these bullets, but it was frightening.'

Carter managed to slip away from the body of men and ran for his life. 'After a short period of freedom, Bill was recaptured and sent to a prisoner of war camp in Germany before being moved on to a coal mine in Silesia where he remained for 18 months before catching pneumonia. He then worked as a forced labourer elsewhere in occupied Europe before escaping in the closing stages of the war before finding refuge with the American army.'[20] He weighed only 7 stone 8 lb when he returned to his home in Dorking, Surrey. He died in 2004.

Bob Brown was also in the byre and watched the surrender, but did not follow the group led by Major Ryder through the stable door. Instead, accompanied by John Hagan and Bill Leven, Brown decided to leave in the opposite direction through a door which opened onto the road.

The smoke from the burning house was going that way, so we thought we'd keep in the smoke as extra cover in the hopes of getting away. We went in the ditch at the side of the road and in the ditch was the adjutant [Captain Long], lying on the ground and the medical officer [Lieutenant Draffin] was there. We attempted to go out of the ditch and cross the road but as we did so the German patrols were coming up from the village of Le Paradis and we just couldn't get over the road. They just shouted, 'Hands up!' or words to that effect and that was that. They pushed and knocked us about a bit but nothing outrageous.

An explanation was given during Knoechlein's trial by Counsel for the Prosecution as he outlined the events leading up to the shooting. It concerned the Rue du Paradis on which Duriez Farm was situated.

This road formed the boundary between the Norfolks and the Royal Scots who had been fighting on the right of the Norfolks. The fact that Battalion Headquarters was more or less on this boundary accounts for the curious events that followed the surrender, for although the Norfolks were attacked by one SS Battalion, most of the survivors were captured by the Company which up to that moment had been fighting the Royal Scots. The other SS Battalion took a number of prisoners, among them Captain Long MC who was Battalion Adjutant. The treatment they received was good, and gave little cause for complaint. Had all the Battalion fallen into their hands the terrible events that followed would not have occurred.

Notes
1. Le Paradis War Crimes Investigation and Trial.
2. Jolly, *The Vengeance of Private Pooley*.
3. Le Paradis War Crimes Investigation and Trial.
4. Jolly, *The Vengeance of Private Pooley*.
5. Le Paradis War Crimes Investigation and Trial.
6. Exhibit 19, Document 1, Le Paradis War Crimes Investigation and Trial.
7. Exhibit 19, Document 4, Le Paradis War Crimes Investigation and Trial.
8. Le Paradis War Crimes Investigation and Trial.
9. Exhibit 19, Document 3, Le Paradis War Crimes Investigation and Trial.
10. Exhibit 19, Document 5, Le Paradis War Crimes Investigation and Trial.
11. Exhibit 19, covering letter from General Staff XVI Corps HQ to Sixth Army HQ, dated 3 June 1940. Le Paradis War Crimes Investigation and Trial.
12. Ailsby, Christopher, *Waffen SS: An Unpublished Record 1923-1945*, Sidgwick & Jackson, 1999.
13. Louis Creton's statement was made before Inspector Henri Gallett of the Béthune Police, who was asked by the War Crimes Investigation Unit to question the farmer on whose land the shooting had taken place.

14. Jolly, *The Vengeance of Private Pooley.*
15. *Ibid.*
16. Le Paradis War Crimes Investigation and Trial.
17. Jolly, *The Vengeance of Private Pooley.*
18. Sebag-Montefiore, *Dunkirk*, Hastings.
19. Exhibit 19, Document 2, Le Paradis War Crimes Investigation and Trial.
20. *Eastern Daily Press*, Thursday, 29 November 2007.

EPILOGUE

'A lesser regiment might never have recovered.'

I**N HIS REPORT ON THE** B**ATTLE** of La Bassée, compiled while a prisoner of war in 1941, Captain Long added the following handwritten note: 'Total prisoners according to careful calculations made in Germany amounted to approx 150 officers and ORs. This included all captured, wounded, stragglers and survivors from 10th May–28th 1940.'

Two Holy Boys, who should have been among the prisoners of war in Germany, were still on the run when Captain Long made his calculations. Near the town of Vitry Le François, which lies about 200 miles south-east of Calais, Ernie Farrow and Leslie Chamberlain, both from the Norfolk market town of Aylsham, had managed to escape from the columns of prisoners during the long march to Germany. Accompanied by a soldier from Nottingham called Hackett, they tramped the 200 miles back to the coast, reaching the Channel near Cap Gris-Nez around 7 August. Unaware of the scale of the disaster, they had clung to the hope that the BEF was still in northern France – but it had been gone for almost two months.

Hackett, unfortunately, was killed in an ambush when the fugitives were betrayed, but with the assistance of the Maquis, Farrow and Chamberlain made their way to Marseilles via Paris. There they were separated when Chamberlain became ill with a stomach complaint. A French girl helped Farrow across the border to Spain where he was captured and imprisoned by the Spanish authorities. He was kept in various gaols for several months until British Embassy officials helped him to Gibraltar. Reunited with Leslie Chamberlain, the two men were brought back to England. Ernie Farrow told the story of his home run to Norfolk author Cyril

Jolly who published the account in 1986 under the title *The Man who Missed the Massacre.*

The BEF had been involved in a brief and tragic campaign, a battle lost. Britain managed to withdraw enough experienced troops with which to rebuild, but this had only been achieved by the sacrifice of others. The Holy Boys had defended their sector of the Canal Line until only a handful of the thousand men who had gone to France were left.

Yet even as their battle ended on that May afternoon in Le Paradis, another battalion of Holy Boys were preparing to fight on. West of the German line, they were cut off from the main body of the BEF and the wide evacuation beaches between Dunkirk and De Panne.

Attached to the 51st Highland Division, 7th Norfolks fought on near Abbeville. But once the BEF had gone and the fighting in the north-eastern sector was over, the Germans could direct their full might onto the remaining Allied forces.

Evacuation through Le Harve was mooted as a possibility, but the port lay at the mercy of German heavy artilleryy. The Highlanders and Holy Boys fell back on the port of St Valéry-en-Caux, which lies midway between Fécamp and Dieppe, and a desperate rearguard was fought while evacuation was awaited. A few survivors were lifted by the Royal Navy during the night 10/11 June, but as the Germans – Rommel's Panzers included – tightened the circle around the port, further evacuation was impossible. On Wednesday, 12 June, Major General Fortune, commander of the 51st Highland Division, was ordered to surrender. Although some 2,280 Allied soldiers were evacuated from Veules-les-Roses, about 4 miles east of St Valéry, the remainder of the men in the Division felt that they had been betrayed and abandoned.

Saul David in his excellent 1994 study of the 51st Highland Division's role in France during 1940 chose an apt title: *Churchill's Sacrifice of the Highland Division.* Sacrificed with them was the 7th Battalion Royal Norfolk Regiment. Some Holy Boys did, however, manage to escape. Thirty-one, under the command of Second Lieutenant Walker, put to sea in a fishing boat and using shovels and planks as oars managed to reach the destroyer HMS *Harvester.*

Those early days of the war were grim for many of the regiments that made up the British Expeditionary Force. Two years later, the Royal Norfolk Regiment was faced with another disaster. When Singapore fell, the 4th, 5th and 6th Battalions were lost and many fine men spent the remainder of the war, or died, under the barbaric and inhumane regime inflicted on their prisoners by the Japanese.

Lieutenant General Sir Brian Horrocks believed that these were a series of disasters

> from which a lesser regiment might never have recovered . . .
> Yet such was their resilience that they had the distinction of
> winning five VCs – more than any other Regiment – and under
> the leadership of their redoubtable commander, Robert Scott,
> the 2nd Battalion played a vital role in the relief of Kohima;
> the desperate battle which saved India from a Japanese
> invasion.[1]

It was during the bitter fighting at Kohima on 6 May 1944 that Captain John Randle posthumously won the second of the Regiment's VCs of the Second World War. Eight months later, on 31 January 1945, at Kangaw on the Arakan coast of Burma, Lieutenant George Knowland, a Norfolk serving in the Commandos, won what was to be the fifth VC.

The men of the 1st Battalion, which had returned from India in 1940, were by 1942 'impatient for an operational role in the war'. Active service appeared 'tantalizingly remote: other infantry formations were leaving for North Africa and India by every tide, but the 1st Royal Norfolks found themselves in Wimbledon, of all improbable and unmilitary places, as part of a Guards Brigade allotted to the defence of the United Kingdom'.[2]

On 6 June 1944, the 1st Battalion finally joined the war when they came ashore in the second wave of troops to land on Sword Beach. On 28 June, the 7th Battalion, no longer pioneers, also landed in Normandy. As the Allies battled to break out, the Holy Boys won the third and fourth of the Regiment's VCs. Corporal Sidney 'Basher' Bates of the 1st Battalion, posthumously, for his courage at Sourdeval on 6 August; and the following day, Captain David Jamieson of the 7th Battalion, for his dauntless leadership at the bridgehead over the River Orne, south of Grimsbosq.

Once the Allies had broken German resistance later that month, a long road across Europe still lay ahead. Sadly, the men of the 7th Battalion never completed that journey as a battalion. With a shortage of manpower and reinforcements needed by many other units, the 59th Division, as the junior division in 21st Army Group, was disbanded and the 7th was dispersed on 22 August 1944. Three of the companies joined other battalions, but seven officers and 180 men did continue to serve under the badge of Britannia when they were moved to the 1st Battalion.

Leading the 1st Royal Norfolks on their slog from Normandy was Lieutenant Colonel Hugh Bellamy. In January 1945, Bellamy left the Holy Boys to command 6 Air Landing Brigade. His successor, who took command on the 19th, was a man who during the bitterly cold winter of 1940 had been the first of the Holy Boys to engage the Germans during the Second World War. Wounded on the Escaut and evacuated to England, he had previously been the Battalion's Second in Command, until he had taken over command of the 4th Battalion The Lincolnshire Regiment in April 1944. Now he had been given the command he coveted most – an almost legendary figure, who Field Marshal Montgomery described as 'my obstinate friend', and of whom the men under his command said that when he shouted an order it could be heard all over France.

In recent years, John Lincoln MC, who served as a lieutenant in the 1st Battalion from D-Day to VE-Day, said of his CO, 'He was told what to do and he did it but I know the loss of life affected him. He was deeply upset.'

His men always had the utmost faith in him. Brave, bloody-minded, a born leader, Lieutenant Colonel Peter Barclay DSO MC saw the Holy Boys to Victory in Europe.

The wheel had come full circle. Barclay had been part of that early struggle to hold back the Nazi advance and he spoke warmly of those who had fought so valiantly during those early, ill-fated months of the Second World War:

> The first thing I'd pay tribute to is the men and the morale that we had in the battalion which was absolutely wonderful. It was the most thrilling feeling to experience the spirit of the

chaps who are with you. It's intangible but it's a most exhilarating potent influence and it's a most wonderful reviver. You can never feel depressed when you've got a spirit round you like the spirit we enjoyed. And the whole thing was treated as a jolly well worthwhile job that had to be done and was going to be done jolly well . . .

We had tremendous courage in our men and the way they held out when the Dunkirk withdrawal was going on, they were stopping the Germans interfering with the withdrawal of thousands and thousands and thousands of other people . . . The Battalion was practically wiped out doing it. Such was the morale and such was the determination to put the biggest possible spanner in the Germans' advance that it succeeded in getting the better part of the BEF back to England. Without that sort of determined stand at Béthune, where they were finally eliminated, there wouldn't have been anything like the number getting away from Dunkirk.

In 1957, the following awards were granted to the 2nd Battalion under the authority of Army Order No. 86: Defence of the Escaut and St Omer-La Bassée – but only the latter was allowed to be borne on the colours.

Officers and men who fought with the various battalions of the Regiment in the Second World War were surprised that some of the places where the fighting had been at its fiercest were, in some cases, not listed. Le Paradis was asked for but the Battle Honours Committee did not approve and awarded St Omer-La Bassée instead.

Notes
1. Lieutenant General Sir Brian Horrocks quoted in Carew, *The Royal Norfolk Regiment*.
2. Carew, *ibid*.

BIBLIOGRAPHY

Books

Ailsby, Christopher, *Waffen SS: An Unpublished Record 1923-1945*, Sidgwick & Jackson, 1999.

Atkin, Ronald, *Pillar of Fire: Dunkirk 1940*, Sidgwick & Jackson, 1990.

Bond, Brian and Taylor, Michael (eds), *The Battle for France and Flanders: Sixty Years On*, Leo Cooper, 2001.

Bond, Brian (ed.), *Chief of Staff: The Diaries of Lieutenant General Sir Henry Pownall*, Leo Cooper, 1972.

Caddick-Adams, Peter, 'The German Breakthrough at Sedan, 12-15 May 1940', in Bond, Brian and Taylor, Michael (eds), *The Battle for France and Flanders*, Leo Cooper, 2001.

Calder, Angus, *The Myth of the Blitz*, Jonathan Cape, 1991.

Carew, Tim, *The Royal Norfolk Regiment*, Royal Norfolk Regimental Association, 1991.

Churchill, W.S., *The Second World War*, vol. II, *Their Finest Hour*, Cassell, 1959.

Colville, Sir John, *The Fringes of Power: Downing Street Diaries 1939-55*, Hodder & Stoughton, 1985.

Danchev, Alex and Todman, Daniel (eds), *War Diaries 1939-1945: Field Marshal Lord Alanbrooke*, Orion, 2002.

Ellis, L.F., *The War in France and Flanders 1939-40*, HMSO, 1953.

Gardiner, W.J.R. (ed.), *The Evacuation from Dunkirk: Operation Dynamo, 26 May to 4 June 1940*, Naval Historical Branch, Ministry of Defence, Naval Staff Histories: series editor, Captain Christopher Page, Frank Cass Publications, 2000.

Gibbs, N.H., *History of the Second World War: The Grand Strategy*, vol. I, HMSO, 1976. Crown copyright material is reproduced with the kind permission of the Controller of the Stationery Office and the Queen's Printer of Scotland.

Harman, Nicholas, *Dunkirk: The Necessary Myth*, Hodder & Stoughton, 1980.

Ismay, Lord, *The Memoirs of Lord Ismay*, Heinemann, 1960.

Jackson, Julian, *The Fall of France: The Nazi Invasion of 1940*, Oxford University Press, 2003.

——, *Dunkirk: The British Evacuation, 1940*, Cassell, 2004.

Jolly, Cyril, *The Man who Missed the Massacre*, published privately by the author, 1986.

——, *The Vengeance of Private Pooley*, Heinemann, 1956. Reproduced by courtesy of the estate of Cyril Jolly.

Keegan, John, *The Second World War*, Hutchinson, 1989.

Kemp, Lieutenant Commander P.K., *History of the Royal Norfolk Regiment 1919-1951*, vol. III, Soman Wherry Press, 1953. Reproduced by kind permission of the Trustees of the Royal Norfolk Rgimental Museum, Norwich.

Long, Captain Charles, 'Report on the Battle of La Bassée Canal, 24-28 May 1940', compiled by Long with the assistance of other officers while POWs at Oflag VIIB, Germany. Reproduced by kind permission of the Trustees of the Royal Norfolk Regimental Museum, Norwich.

MacLeod, R. and Kelly, Denis (eds), *The Ironside Diaries*, Constable, 1962.

McGeoch, Angus, *The Third Reich at War*, Veranov, Michael (ed.), Magpie Books, an imprint of Constable & Robinson, 2004.

Mellenthin, Major General F.W. von, *Panzer Battles*, Tempus, 2000. Reproduced by kind permission of the History Press.

Montgomery, Field Marshal The Viscount, of Alamein, KG, *Memoirs*, Pen & Sword, 2007, by kind permission of A.P. Watt on behalf of Viscount Montgomery of Alamein.

Murray Brown, Lieutenant Colonel C.R., DSO, *Britannia Magazine*, No. 27, reproduced by kind permission of the Royal Norfolk Regimental Museum, Norwich.

Ripley, Tim, *Hitler's Praetorians: The History of the Waffen SS 1925-1945*, Spellmount, 2004. Reproduced by kind permission of The History Press.

Pallaud, John-Paul, *Blitzkrieg in the West, Then and Now*, Battle of Britain Prints, 1991.

Sarkar, Dilip, *Guards VC: Blitzkrieg 1940*, Ramrod Publications, 1999.

Williamson, Gordon, *The SS: Hitler's Instrument of Terror*, Sidgwick & Jackson, 1994.

Imperial War Museum Sound Archives

Barclay, Peter – Interview (Accession No. 008192/07).

Boast, Denis – Interview (Accession No. 17535).

Brough, Arthur – Interview (Accession No. 16972).

Brown, Bob – Interview (Accession No. 10393/3).
Farrow, Ernie – Interview (Accession No. 11479/5).
Gilding, Walter – Interview (Accession No. 17534).
Leggett, Ernie – Interview (Accession No. 17761).
Lines, Herbert – Interview (Accession No. 17297).
Seymour, Bill – Interview (Accession No. 17672).